Yugoslavia

ria

Apulia

Greece

Turkey

Syria

Peloponnese

Cyprus

Lebanon

Crete

Israel

ibya

Egypt

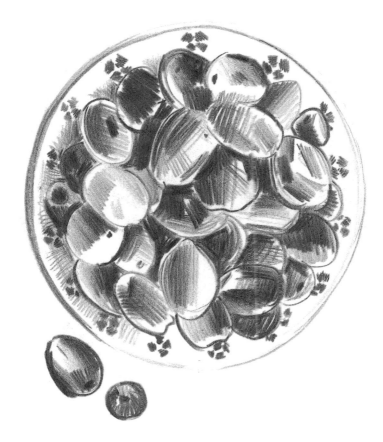

THE ESSENTIAL

OLIVE

O · I · L

Companion

ANNE DOLAMORE

SALEM HOUSE PUBLISHERS
Topsfield, Massachusetts

Designed and produced by Grub Street,
London

First published in the United States by Salem
House Publishers, 1989,
462 Boston Street, Topsfield, Massachusetts,
01983.

Art Director: Roger Hammond
Designer: Deborah George

Library of Congress Cataloguing in Publication
Data:
Catalogue Card No. 88–61761

ISBN: 0-88162-396-2

Typeset by Chapterhouse, Formby, England

Printed in the UK by
Maclehose and Partners

ACKNOWLEDGEMENTS

My greatest debt of gratitude is to
Alicia Rios, whose wonderful talk
on this subject first inspired me to learn
more. Her generosity with information
and recipes and her hospitality have
made this book possible. Thanks to
Charles Carey of The Oil Merchant for
his infectious enthusiasm and advice.
Clare Marsden of Carbonell for her kind
and ready help. Senor Moya of ASOLIVA
for his friendliness and assistance. Marie
Jose Sevilla, of Foods from Spain, for
allowing me to use some of her delicious
recipes. The International Olive Oil
Council, in Madrid, for a wealth of useful
information.

Special thanks to John Davies of
Grub Street for his belief in the book and
invaluable support. Roger Hammond for
his patient artistic expertise. To
Madeleine, for her beautiful drawings,
without which the book would lack so
much.

To all the producers and growers,
who gave so readily of their time and
wisdom. To all my friends, who have
seen me through my ups and downs,
always offering encouragement, but
especially Jenny, for providing home
comforts and genial company, Graeme
for laughter and distraction, PJ for
always being generous in times of need.
And Rosemary Russell, who has
provided more than she will ever realize.

To Tino, for ten happy years.

CONTENTS

INTRODUCTION

*W*hen I first mentioned to friends, last year, that I was writing a book about olive oil, most of them stared at me with incredulity, and after a pause said, 'oh you mean Popeye's girlfriend'! This shows how little the golden juice of the olive still means to non-Mediterraneans. I'm sure, that had I said this in France, Italy or Greece, people would have immediately and correctly assumed I was talking about one of the basic commodities of their everyday life.

When initial surprise at my choice of subject had passed, the next comment was invariably, 'goodness, is there much to say about olive oil'. The answer, I hope, will become apparent on further reading.

What has now become for me a consuming passion, in all senses, started in 1986 at the Oxford Symposium on Food. This is an annual event, where food historians, cookery writers and interested parties such as myself, gather to exchange ideas, present and listen to papers on a given topic. The whole affair is a wonderful medley of the serious and funny, the popular and the erudite, and of course we eat and drink! It is a very convivial gathering, where you make new friends and greet old ones, and if we are fortunate enough to be blessed with fine weather, the rolling lawns of St Anthony's College provide an idyllic setting for more informal chats. The Symposium in its present form has been running since 1981, established by Alan Davidson and Theodore Zeldin, to whom the culinary fraternity owe much for creating this fertile forum.

The author in a market in Meknes

At the Symposium in 1986, Alicia Rios gave one of the most entertaining talks I have ever attended on any subject. Her wit and enthusiasm were infectious. She made me realize that olive oil was not just something to cook with, but a precious gift. With a history as old as time, it has a variety of organoleptic experiences that no other fruit, apart from the grape, can ever match. When I tasted the different oils she presented, it was like my first taste of really fine wine. I was converted.

So I started just for my personal interest, to research the subject. What began as curiosity has ended in a book! I discovered at the outset that all the pieces were there, but no one had pulled them together. It is truly amazing that with so much written about the grape, there was so little about its historical peer — the olive. The subject has proved vaster than I ever imagined when I embarked on my quest.

What I have come to realize is how important the seemingly humble olive was in the formation of empires. How deeply rooted in legend and folklore it is and how many communities rely on its very existence for their livelihood.

The joy for me is that many of my favourite places are linked by the olive and it has been delightful to journey to countries, not just as a tourist, but with a specific mission — a mission which has taken me to venues I would never otherwise have visited and introduced me to people I would never have met. The more I have become immersed in my theme, the more compulsive it has become.

The first seeds of my interest in things gastronomic had been sown by my godfather, who taught me the joys of good food, good wine and classical music. For this I owe him eternal thanks. To have revealed at such a tender age the finer things of life, is an education indeed.

Since those first tentative steps on the culinary road, I have proceeded along a fascinating path of discovery. I started travelling seriously after leaving University, at which point I began to appreciate the delights of simple, well prepared food — a grilled fish in a Greek island taverna, a boeuf en daube in a French lorry driver's cafe, tapas and a glass of fino in a village bar in Spain, the street food in Egypt and Morocco, fresh pasta in Italy, or a breakfast of fresh bread and creamy yoghurt in Turkey.

You get near to the heart of a country when you sample its food, and you truly begin to understand the people when you wander into their markets and see how they shop. You may visit the monuments and marvel at the architecture in the Mediterranean to put you in touch with its glorious past, but the present is lived round these market stalls and the harbours where the latest catch has been landed.

Writing this book has given me the opportunity to deepen this education. It has been a wonderful, exciting odyssey. It is a strange path that leads one to discover a topic of interest and to find, that it stimulates you sufficiently to want to share the excitement with other people. If I can persuade you in the following pages to follow my voyage of discovery, I promise you will not be disappointed.

THE OLIVE AND THE ANCIENT WORLD

The whole Mediterranean,
the sculpture, the palms, the gold beads, the
bearded heroes, the wine, the ideas, the
ships, the moonlight, the winged gorgons, the
bronze men, the philosophers, all of it seems
to rise in the sour, pungent taste of these
black olives between the teeth. A taste older
than meat, older than wine. A taste as old as
cold water.

LAWRENCE DURRELL. *PROSPERO'S CELL*

Detail from an amphora in the British Museum

*T*he history of the olive weaves its way through myths and legends, wars and treaties, commerce and culture, theology, medicine and gastronomy. Its precise origins are lost back in the mists of time. However, the olive could be viewed as a genuine bench mark of civilisation itself. While primitive man was hunting and scavenging, while he was nomadic, he didn't plough to cultivate crops; only when he was settled and creative, did he have time for planting trees and building palaces and temples. So it's not surprising to find the olive figuring as prominently as it does in Egyptian, Greek and Roman history.

Who first discovered the uses of the olive, and how to extract its unctuous oil no-one really knows. The remarkable fact is that the green olive is inedible in its natural state; it needs to be treated with water or brine to remove the bitter glucosides. So did man come to discover the delights of the olive by eating ripe, black fruit or did he one day gather olives which had fallen into the sea at the water's edge?

There are indications that it was first cultivated in Syria by a Semitic race, 6000 years ago, for records show that Ancient Palestine was famous for its olive groves, and exported oil to the Ancient Egyptians.

The Room of the Olive Press at Knossos

The Bible, not surprisingly, contains many references to the culinary and religious uses of olives and olive oil. In the *Book of Genesis* the dove sent out from the ark by Noah returned with an olive branch. Here it became the great symbol of peace, indicating the end of God's anger. And its recognition by Noah, suggests that it was already a well known tree.

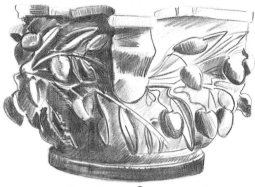

Ancient Roman vase with olive motif

The greatest religious significance of olive oil is documented in the *Book of Exodus*, where Moses is told by the Lord how to make an anointing oil of spices and olive oil. During consecration, holy anointing oil was poured over the heads of kings and priests, and it is still used today in the Roman Catholic Church, at baptisms and in the last rites for the dying.

The sacred use of olive oil also extended into the preparation of food used during sacrifices, such as pure wheatmeal flour kneaded with olive oil, which is mentioned in the *Book of Leviticus*.

Another reference showing how important olive oil was in Biblical times is given in the *Book of Judges* The trees wanted to elect a king to rule over them and so they chose the olive tree but the tree refused saying 'and give up my oil by which gods and men are honoured and go to sway over the trees?'

The olive has had great significance for every religion, though, and the Koran contains this wonderful passage, 'Allah is the light of the heavens and of the earth. His light is like a niche wherein a lamp is to be found, the lamp is in a glass cover which seems to be a twinkling star; it is lit thanks to a sacred tree: the olive tree, which has an oil so clear that it would give light even if no spark were put to it.'

There is speculation that the olive may have appeared first west of the Nile Delta, as the Ancient Egyptians certainly knew how to grow olives. Or it may have been introduced into Egypt by the Hyksos, a Semitic tribe, who invaded Upper Egypt around 1650BC, and remained for about 100 years before being driven out by the Egyptian king, Amosis. Its commerce is mentioned in Egyptian records, olives are depicted in tomb paintings and branches have been found in sarcophagi. Garlands of olive branches even crowned the head of Tutankhamun.

It was the goddess Isis, wife of the supreme god Osiris, who was praised for giving the Egyptians the necessary knowledge to cultivate the trees and produce oil. But their olive oil production never subsequently matched that of the Greeks and Romans. Though the Egyptians used olive oil for cooking and medicine, it is noted in Greek records as being of poor quality, and so they imported olive oil from Syria and Crete.

Inscribed earthenware tablets dating back to 2500BC, from Crete at the time of King Minos, are some of the oldest surviving references to olive oil. They mention different types of oil as well as the uses made of it. The palace at Knossos was the centre of economic life and contained a chamber known as The Room of the Olive Press. Hundreds of the great amphorae, some standing nearly five feet high, in which olive oil was stored, can still be seen today.

At the height of Cretan trading with the islands of the eastern Mediterranean and Egypt, these amphorae, some of which contained wine as well as olive oil, represented Minoan currency.

Following the collapse of Cretan power in 1200BC, the Phoenicians became the masters of trade in the Mediterranean, Tyre being the commercial capital. About this time, the Phoenicians taught the Greeks to use oil as a source of light and to make the terracotta lamps necessary to burn oil. By the 5th century BC, the Greeks and Phoenicians were major exporters of olive oil and the olive had been introduced to the shores of the western Mediterranean countries, on the course of their trading routes to Spain.

The olive must have occurred naturally in Greece, however, because the Greeks gave it their own name — *elaia*. If it had been introduced from Syria, they would have adopted the Hebrew, *zayit*, or *zeit*, as it became in the Arabic countries of North Africa.

Greek legend records a famous story which accounts for one

supposed origin of the olive. There was a contest between the goddess, Pallas Athene and Poseidon for control of the land of Attica. Zeus promised the land to the one who provided the most useful gift. Poseidon struck the ground with his trident and a magnificent horse sprung forth. Athene produced an olive tree and was judged victorious. It is understandable that Athene should have won the contest, since olive oil provides so much vital to life; it is a food, a medicine and a source of light. From her Athens took its name, and this allegory is no doubt why some historians credit Greece as the true source of the olive.

The Greeks also connected Aristeus, the son of Apollo and the nymph Cyrene with the discovery of the olive, since he was a god of husbandry. In another legend, Acropos, the founder of Athens was hailed for teaching the Greeks how to extract olive oil on learning of the olive from Aristeus.

Olive grove on a stormy spring afternoon

Indeed, Herodotus later described Athens, in the 5th century BC, as the centre of Greek olive growing. Oil was produced in such abundance that it became one of her major exports. In fact, so important did olive culture become to the Greeks and their economy, that olive groves were considered sacred ground and only virgins and chaste men were allowed to cultivate them.

In the 6th century BC, Solon, the famous statesman and poet, introduced laws protecting the olive trees of Athens. Anyone caught cutting down trees was executed. Even today in countries where the olive tree is pre-eminent, one of the cruellest things to say about someone, is that they are the kind of person who would cut down an olive tree.

Subsequently, victors in the ancient Greek games were rewarded with wreaths of olives; and at the Olympic games, this garland of olive branches was cut from the sacred tree of the Acropolis, the legendary tree of Pallas Athene.

The Greek calendar was full of festivals featuring athletic events. One of the most important was the Great Panathenia, at which the victors received the prize of a jar full of olive oil known today as a Panathenic amphora.

After the destruction of the Acropolis and its venerable olive tree by Xerxes, leader of the Persian invasion force in 480BC, when the whole of Athens lay in ruins, on the first evening; it is said that the tree of the Temple of Erechteum — the original temple of the Athenian deities — sprouted forth once again; an eternal symbol of fertility.

The olive spread still further throughout the Mediterranean, with the expansion of the Roman

Amphorae for storing oil

Empire. The Carthaginians had introduced olives to what is now Tunisia but after the Romans invaded the country and destroyed Carthage, they planted olives from Tripoli, n Libya, to Algeria. True, the olive tree grew in North Africa before the Romans arrived, but they were responsible for spreading it through the area.

Roman legends credit the goddess Minerva, closely related to the figure of Pallas Athene, as a goddess of peace and wisdom, with giving the Romans the art of cultivating the olive tree. The wild olive tree is attributed to Hercules however, who struck the ground with his mighty club and it took root. Moreover, it was under an olive tree that the twins, Romulus and Remus, legendary founders of Rome, rescued from the Tiber and suckled by the she-wolf, were supposed to have been born.

Greek and Roman literature abounds with references to olives and olive oil. Virgil, in the *Georgics*, sings the praises of the olive tree and its rich fruit; Ovid, in the *Metamorphoses* depicts Beaucis preparing a meal with olive oil for her heavenly guests; Plutarch recalls the profit the oil from Numidia gave to Caesar; in the 1st century BC, Cato in his *Treatise on Agriculture* gives a detailed list of the equipment necessary for growing an olive tree; and Pliny the Elder, whose famous maxim for a happy life recommended the use of wine inside and oil outside, in his *Natural History* warns 'the worst possible accident that can happen to the olive is that it rains when the tree blooms because of the risk of blossom drop'.

Some beautiful works of art survive today which depict scenes from olive harvests and oil pressing. In the British Museum, there is an amphora which shows men with sticks knocking down olives on to sheets spread or the ground below. Today, in many parts of the Mediterranean, olives are gathered in identical fashion. Amphorae were used for the transportation of oil all over Europe, and the seal on the amphora served the same purpose as a label does today; it gave the name of the producer by three initials, the grove, the name of the trader and in symbols the taxes paid on the oil. Centuries-old murals, frescos and mosaics can be found wherever olives were grown and they stand as a testament to how little methods of pressing and harvesting have changed over thousands of years.

THE OLIVE TREE

'**If I could paint and had the necessary time, I should devote myself for a few years to making pictures only of olive trees. What a wealth of variations upon a single theme.**'

ALDOUS HUXLEY. *THE OLIVE TREE*.

*T*he wild olive tree (Oleaster) grew, and still grows, in most of the Mediterranean countries, but this species bears meagre fruit. The Olea Europaea, on the other hand, which is the domesticated variety, is not known in the wild. How the domesticated clone came to be developed is a mystery, but the most likely possibility is that in ancient times, certain trees were noted for being particularly prolific in their production of fruit. These were then probably cultivated by means of cuttings and so, over hundreds of years, plantations of vigorous, abundant trees were established.

The olive belongs to the family of Oleales, flowering plants of which the lilac, jasmin and oleander are also members. The Olea

Europaea species is divided into three sub-species: Olea Europaea
Euromediterranea: sativa; oleaster; Laperrini: typica var;
cyrenaica var; maireana var; Cuspidata: varied.

The Olea Euromediterranea sativa or Olea sativa HOFFM and
LINK is also known as the cultivated olive tree; there are literally
hundreds of varieties and like the grape, the variety grown
depends on the climate, the soil and also whether the olives are to
be pressed for oil or preserved for eating. With table olives, it is
firmness and fleshiness of fruit which is important whereas olives
grown for pressing must have a high oil content. There is no
difference in the varieties of green and black olives, for all olives
are green at first and turn black when fully ripe, changing through
a beautiful spectrum of colours; rose, wine-rose, brown, deep
violet, deep chestnut, reddish black, and finally violet black. Some
olives, such as the Spanish Manzanilla and the French Picholine,
are tastier when picked green, others such as the famous, tiny
Nicois and the Greek Kalamata, are best when fully ripe.

The olive tree cannot tolerate extreme cold or damp but can
survive lengthy periods of drought. So it is chiefly to be found
between the latitudes 25° and 45° North, and it especially
flourishes in the Mediterranean climate, with its mild winters and
long hot summers.

The tree can grow to a great height, as much as 50ft but most
are pruned, so they remain at about half this, to facilitate picking.

Its trunk, which is smooth and grey when young, becomes
twisted and knarled with the years. It takes about five to eight
years before an olive tree will bear its first fruit and then it can go
on producing for years and years. Olive trees have a great tenacity
of life because when the main trunk dies, new shoots sprout up
around its base, eventually growing into a new tree. It is not
unusual, for instance, for olive trees to live to 600 years or more.
So it is not impossible that the trees at present in the Garden of
Gethsemane could be those under which Christ prayed, the night
before he died.

New trees can be grown from seed but they take years to
reach the fruit-bearing stage, the most common method of
propagation being to take cuttings from mature trees. Some
varieties or cultivars have developed resistance to cold, others to

pests and drought. The advantage of propagation from cuttings is that the new tree will carry these resistances.

The tree is an evergreen and its leaves live for about three years, before dying and making way for new ones. Olive leaves are paired opposite each other down the branches. They are single and undivided, rather like a willow leaf, lance-shaped, shiny and leathery. The upper surface is dark green and the lower surface appears to be a silvery-green, because it is covered with minute scales. This is why in the wind, olive trees seem to shimmer in a silvery haze.

The tree blooms in late spring with clusters of white flowers. Depending on the variety, there can be anything from ten to over forty flowers in a cluster, but only one in every twenty flowers will become an olive. Even though olive trees are self-pollinating, it is very difficult for the flowers to achieve fertilization at the best of times, but the weather is the prime enemy. Rain at blossom time can be disastrous. As a result, fruit setting is erratic but it is improved by planting another variety of olive tree for cross-pollination.

Between June and October fruition takes place. This is the time during which the stone (endocarp) hardens and the pulp (mesocarp) fills out. The flesh is encased by the skin (epicarp) and as the olive ripens the epicarp changes from green through violet and red to black. Six to eight months after the blossoms appear, the olives have maximum oil content; they are black and fully ripe.

The olive is a stone fruit, like the cherry or plum, and it is the slender stone encased inside the fruit which contains the seed of the tree itself. Botanically this type of fleshy fruit encasing a stone is known as a drupe from the Greek, Δρυππα, meaning an overripe, wrinkled olive.

Olive trees are mostly found in arid terrain; they need little rain and can survive in the poorest soils because the roots bore deep into the earth in search of what little moisture they require. In these conditions, they will produce a mediocre harvest. However, with care and attention the tree is far more productive and bears fruit every year, rather than every other year.

Growing olives is now big business; olive oil is a world

commodity, so modern methods of cultivation are being used increasingly, much like other vital crops — and these days on most commercial estates trees are fertilised, pruned and irrigated.

In early autumn and spring, the soil in the groves is ploughed and weeded and the trees are pruned. Pruning is a most important but labour intensive process; by thinning out the growth on the crown of the tree, the fruit-bearing branches can be exposed to sun and air. The removal of vigorous but sterile branches and suckers, which appear in abundance at the base of the tree, means that the nutrients in the soil will be better utilised. A tree can yield between 15 and 20 kilos (approximately 8–25lbs) of olives depending on how it is tended. Think of the work involved in going over every tree, laboriously and carefully one at at time by hand. There can be no short cuts, and there is no possible means of mechanised pruning.

Like all fruit trees, the olive is subject to attack from fungi and insects. Its particular enemy is the olive moth, whose caterpillars will happily eat their way through leaves and buds. These enemies need to be controlled, and so spraying with pesticides may also be one of the duties of the olive producer. However, some producers choose to grow their olives organically because of concern over contamination of the fruit by pesticides.

The olive grower's year is certainly a full and active one. Apart from pruning and fertilising, he has to harvest and press the olives.

The desired object of all this work is, of course, to produce a good crop of olives but the bounty which the olive tree provides is not in its fruit alone; there is almost no part of this eternal tree which man cannot utilize.

Olive wood, for example, is highly regarded for its beautiful black and brown grain and its honey colour. Indeed, so highly did the Romans value it, that they forbad its being burned for common use and reserved it solely for the altars of the gods. It is now fashioned into furniture, boxes, salad bowls and today, as in Greek times, is used by craftsmen and women for carving works of art.

Remarkably, the leaves of the olive tree have always been regarded as curative when boiled in water and taken as an infusion. This infusion is recommended for sufferers of hypertension and those with heart conditions, as well as being an effective diuretic. Even the residue of stones and skins after pressing, is used in many mills as fuel, and may also be used as fertilizer for the trees. Can there be another tree with such a history, with such folklore surrounding it and with such a multiplicity of uses?

Winter landscape

THE FRUIT OF THE TREE

'He causeth the grass to grow for the cattle, and plants for the service of man: That he may bring forth food out of the earth; and wine that maketh glad the heart of man, and oil to make his face shine . . .'

PSALMS.

*G*oing out to buy olive oil today, you are presented with an exciting but perhaps bewildering choice in supermarkets, wine shops and delicatessens. There are virgin oils, and pure oils from Spain, Italy, France, and Greece. There are single estate oils and national brands as well as own brands from the large multiples. There are emerald green oils and golden yellow oils. Bottles and tins of all shapes, sizes and designs. So where does someone start to make a selection?

Olive oil, like wine has an enormous diversity of flavours. The taste, colour and aroma is dependent on the country of origin, the soil on which the trees are grown, the variety of olive and the method of harvesting. There are also different qualities which are reflected in the price, but the information on the label will help you make an informed choice.

Cold pressed, extra virgin olive oil is the best you can buy. Virgin oil will vary in taste and colour from year to year because it is the pure, unadulterated juice of the olive. Unlike wine however, olive oil does not improve with age. It is at its best the year after pressing. The colour gives no indication of its quality because if the olives are green when they are harvested the oil will be different to the oil from black, ripe olives. Olive oils have a range of colours from deep green to light gold and as many flavours, from pungent and peppery to the light and fruity. It's all a matter of personal taste, but you may find that the extra virgin oils are best used for dressing salads and adding uncooked to certain dishes such as soup because of their powerful flavours. They come into their own when used in regional dishes where the flavour of the local olive oil gives the dish its intrinsic taste; a dish of ratatouille from Provence, a bowl of pasta from Italy, a luscious tagine from Morocco — they all owe their distinctiveness to the local olive.

Pure olive oils, which are the refined oils blended with virgin oil to give flavour, colour and aroma, are lighter in flavour and are excellent for making dishes where you don't want the taste to be so strong as to dominate the other ingredients — as with mayonnaise, or for frying.

National brands of pure olive oil such as Carbonell, Sasso, Berio, Bertolli and Cypressa or supermarket own brands, because they are refined and blended will have the same flavour each time you buy a bottle.

To understand the differences in virgin oils and refined oils, it helps to know what happens to the olive once it has been plucked from the tree.

For those who know and love the Mediterranean, summer is the time associated with the riches of fresh figs, aromatic herbs and

Young tree

fragrant melons but in the olive-growing areas the harvest begins in autumn, and then the air is heavy with the delicious smell of the pressed olives.

Picking can start in September and may go on until March, depending on the country and whether the olives are being picked green, or black, for eating, or for oil. In the course of the harvest, the pickers will go back to a tree time and time again, to gather olives at the same stage of ripeness. The groves come alive at harvest time, with small groups spreading out huge nets under the trees to catch the fruit, and women and children crouching under the trees, collecting the olives that have already fallen. It is arduous work but there is a diligent camaraderie.

Harvesting methods have changed very little since the scenes depicted on the ancient amphorae, and hand picking is still the only way to ensure that the fruit is picked at its optimum ripeness and also to prevent bruising. If there were no other considerations, the simple contemplation of every olive being picked individually by hand should be enough to quell the complaints of those who say that olive oil or table olives are expensive.

The hand picker stands on a ladder, with a net slung like a hammock below, slowly and methodically pulling the olives off and dropping them into the net. Poles are used in many places to beat the branches, and the falling fruit is collected in the nets laid out underneath the trees. This is, of course, a practise which dates back to ancient times but there is always the risk of the fruit getting damaged.

Spanish olive pickers

Consequently, other harvesting methods have been developed and research continues in an attempt to mechanize the costly hand-picking. There are tractors with claws which grasp the trunk of the tree and shake the fruit down, by means of vibration, but again though this has undoubtedly helped speed up the harvest, it is not ideal because of possible damage and the trees still have to be gone over after by hand, to remove the stubborn hangers on.

After picking, the olives are gathered into straw baskets and loaded into a waiting trailer, by means of a small elevator, which shakes off the leaves and twigs.

If the grower is also an olive oil producer, the olives will be taken to his mill but

Traditional French oil mill

in most cases the olives are grown by families on small farms, and so the olives are taken to the local co-operative mill. At the co-operative, the farmer's load is weighed and he is given a receipt. He may, if he is a very small producer, collect his oil when his olives have been pressed, or if the co-operative sells to a large company which bottles and markets oil, then he will be paid for his harvest.

Most progress has been made with the automation of the local mills, where anything up to six deliveries can be handled at one time. The mill is worked by a lone individual sitting at a display panel, while a computer whirrs away quietly in the background, weighing, sorting, and washing the incoming harvest.

Vast elevators spirit the olives towards huge hoppers, discarding leaves and earth on the way, to where jets of cold water remove all traces of any impurities.

The olives are not usually stored for long before this sorting and washing begins, certainly no more than a few days and in most cases just a few hours — piles of olives generate heat which induces fermentation, and this impairs the flavour of the resulting

oil. A certain amount of storage can
be beneficial because the heat
generated, if not left for long enough
to start fermentation, will help to
release more oil.

Then the grinding or trituration
begins when the olives are crushed
still with their stones, to shred the
flesh and release the oil — though
in some places today, the stones are
removed first.

The basic principles of milling
are the same today as they were
long ago. Before any machinery was
invented to do the job, the olives
were crushed under foot, just like
grapes, but, of course, without the

*Ancient North African
screw press*

use of any pressure the amount of oil extracted from the olives
was small.

Later on, with the appearance of the wooden lever press,
which is depicted on a Roman mosaic dating back to the 3rd
century BC, and was a construction rather like a giant wooden
nutcracker, in which the olives were squeezed whole to release
the oil without prior crushing, olive oil was extracted under
pressure.

The Roman's screw press was the real breakthrough. This
crushes the fruit between two stone plates drawn together by the
action of the screw, and thus extracts the maximum oil.

Ancient oil mills were circular stone vats, in which a huge
vertical circular mill-stone, fixed at the centre by a wooden shaft,
was drawn round the circumference by men or mules. Later, there
were modifications to this type of mill — they were either two
vertical mill stones linked by a horizontal shaft, or four cone-
shaped rollers set at right angles, driven by steam. Today, in some
small villages, these traditional mills are still in use; in Spain they
are known as Almazara, and in France as Moulin, but where the
old has made way for the new, the mill stones now decorate the
entrances to many of the estates like faithful old retainers.

Separating olives from the twigs and leaves

Now as then, once the olives are crushed, the resulting paste is spread onto loosely woven hemp mats. These are stacked, up to fifty at a time, interspersed with metal discs, which help to distribute the pressure evenly in the press, where they undergo hundreds of tons of weight in an hydraulic press. Today where this form of pressing is still in use (but is becoming rarer), the mats are usually made of nylon rather than esparto. The mats allow the oil to drain through while holding back more solid matter. At this stage, the oil contains some of the fruit's own water. Traditionally, the liquid then flowed into tanks or troughs where the oil was

Hand picking at harvest time

Early North African oil mill

allowed to settle. Being less dense than the water, the oil rises to the surface and can be decanted off. Centuries ago the oil was subsequently stored in sealed amphorae, which protected it from bright sunlight.

Sadly, the romance and simplicity of old-style milling and pressing has now all but gone, and when you visit a modern mill you see very little but bright stainless steel equipment worked by electricity and controlled by computer, occupying only a few square meters of space. The washed olives disappear into a hopper at one end and the oil emerges at the other, the whole process being continuous. However, one can't deny that progress has brought about a superior quality olive oil, produced under the most hygienic conditions. It really is a totally natural product untouched by human hands.

Today, there is no need to spread kilos of paste on mats and stack them in a press. Once the olives are crushed the paste moves into a cylindrical trough, where blades turn the mixture over and over to form a homogeneous mass. This is called malaxation.

The oil is separated from the paste by means of centrifugation, which simply means spinning the paste round at high speed. These modern methods are all adaptations of the old principles, simply taken to the degree of sophistication necessary to ensure the profitable production of olive oil in today's world.

Olive oil produced by these methods is known as first cold pressed olive oil. It is made usually from green, unripe olives which have been pressed once and to which no heat or chemicals have been applied and it takes about 5 kilos of olives to make 1 litre of oil. Except for centrifuging and perhaps filtering, the oil remains untreated. No other vegetable oil is edible just being pressed. All other seed oils have to be treated first because they contain toxins or are not suitable for human consumption in their natural state.

First cold pressed olive oil is a totally pure product and it retains all its natural flavours. Because of this it is possible to recognize the origin of the oil, just as wine can be identified by its intrinsic organoleptic qualities.

These first cold pressed oils are virgin oils, graded according to their acidity in standards set down by the International Olive Oil Council. Approximately 65–90% of oil extracted is virgin olive oil and is ready for consumption.

Olive oil produced by the same natural methods but which because of excessive acidity, colour or flavour is not fit for consumption, is known as lampante virgin olive oil. Such oil needs to be refined, which is done by neutralisation, bleaching and deodorisation.

In the production of first cold pressed olive oil, solid matter known as residue remains and still contains a certain amount of oil. This is mixed with water and heated to 70°C, and is pressed again, yielding an oil of lesser quality and higher acidity. A somewhat similar grade is obtained from bruised fruit. Pressing can be repeated once or twice, yielding each time a poorer grade. At the last press, oil is extracted from the residue with carbon disulphide, more recently with trichlorethylene to yield olive residue oil.

These crude residue oils are very highly coloured, have a strong taste and are very high in acidity. They cannot be marketed simply as olive oil. In this state they are unfit for consumption but, like lampante virgin olive oil, can be treated for sale as 'refined olive-residue oil' — or, when mixed with virgin olive oil, as 'refined olive-residue oil and olive oil'. Olive residue oils that are too high in acidity are used for industrial purposes such as wool combing in the textile industry, in the manufacture of toilet preparations and in making high quality castile soap.

The process of refining the olive oil can be a chemical or a physical process. In the chemical process, caustic soda is added to the oil to draw out the fatty acids. In the physical process, which is being used increasingly, olive oil is put in a drum, which is heated up in a vacuum, to about 180°C. This evaporates the fatty acids and they are drawn off. In this way the oil is neutralised and deodorised.

Another physical method of refining is to use a centrifuge. This is a cheaper process and therefore oils with a very high acidity are centrifuged first. This drives off the greater part of the free fatty acids and the oil can then be treated in the vacuum, to remove the rest.

THE PROCESS OF PRODUCING OLIVE OIL

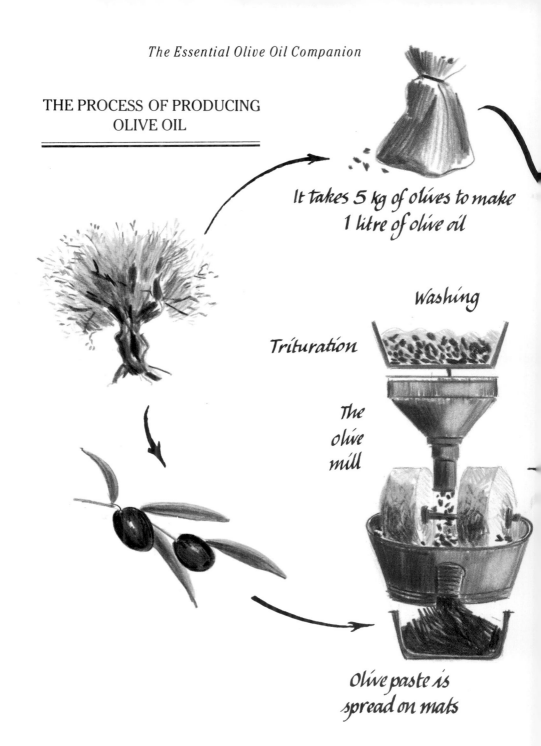

It takes 5 kg of olives to make
1 litre of olive oil

Washing

Trituration

The
olive
mill

Olive paste is
spread on mats

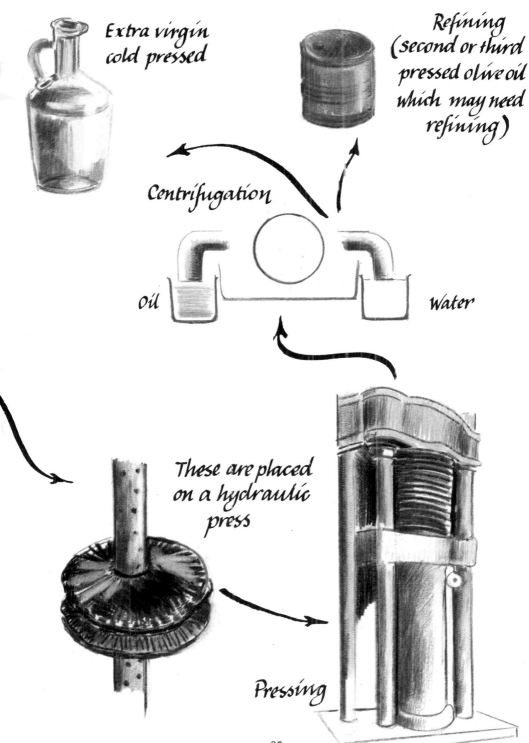

Extra virgin
cold pressed

Refining
(second or third
pressed olive oil
which may need
refining)

Centrifugation

Oil

Water

These are placed
on a hydraulic
press

Pressing

Bleaching to remove the colour is the next process in refining. The oil is first run through a sand, whose properties attract that part of the oil which gives it its colour. Then it is filtered to remove any particles of sand which may remain.

In Spain, Italy, France, Greece and Tunisia, research is going on constantly to improve all the various processes of milling and refining. In 1970 a Centre for the Improvement and Demonstration of Olive Oil Extraction Methods was set up in Cordoba, Spain, for the benefit of all olive oil producers. There is also an experimental oil mill at Seville in Spain called the Instituto de la Grasa y sus Derivados. Places such as these strive to make olive oil production more efficient and cost effective in the face of rising labour costs. The development of the continuous centrifuge method of extraction, for example, has obviated the need for pressing mats which are used in the hydraulic presses and which, because they are made today from synthetic materials derived from petroleum, have become expensive to produce.

Olive oil is a world commodity like wheat, sugar or cocoa and as such its production and labelling is controlled by international legislation and it is this which provides the consumer with assurances on quality.

The first International Olive Oil Agreement was drawn up in 1959, and is administered by the International Olive Oil Council (IOOC), whose headquarters are in Madrid. This council sits twice a year and comprises all olive oil producing countries and olive oil importing members. The EEC is a member, along with Algeria, Egypt, Libya, Morocco, Tunisia, Turkey and Yugoslavia.

The current Olive Oil Agreement came into force in 1979 as an extended and amended version of the 1959 Agreement, and it basically seeks to promote the expansion of the world market by encouraging the improvement of olive oil productivity. It also sets down standards for all of the categories of olive oil. A label reproducing the IOOC emblem, the use of which is governed by regulations, guarantees to the consumer the purity and quality.

The designation 'olive oil' is given to the oil obtained solely from the fruit of the olive tree, to the exclusion of oils obtained using solvents or re-esterification processes, or any mixtures with oils of other kinds.

GRADES OF OLIVE OIL AS DESIGNATED BY THE INTERNATIONAL OLIVE OIL COUNCIL

VIRGIN OLIVE OIL is the oil obtained from the fruit of the olive tree solely by mechanical or other physical means under conditions, and particularly thermal conditions, that do not lead to alterations in the oil. Further, the olive has not undergone any treatment other than washing, centrifugation and filtration.

Virgin Olive Oil fit for consumption as it is, is classified into:

EXTRA VIRGIN OLIVE OIL. This is virgin olive oil of absolutely perfect taste and odour having maximum acidity in terms of oleic acid of 1 gram per 100 grams, or more simply with an acidity of less than 1%.

FINE VIRGIN OLIVE OIL. Virgin olive oil of absolutely perfect taste and odour having a maximum acidity, in terms of oleic acid of 1.5 grams per 100 grams, or acidity of less than 1.5%.

SEMI-FINE OLIVE OIL (or ordinary virgin olive oil) is virgin olive oil of good taste and odour, having a maximum acidity in terms of oleic acid, of 3 grams per 100 grams, with a margin of tolerance of 10% of acidity indicated, in other words a maximum acidity of 3%.

Virgin olive oil not fit for consumption as it is, is designated **VIRGIN OLIVE OIL LAMPANTE** (lamp oil). This is an off-taste and/or off-smelling virgin olive oil or an oil with an acidity in terms of oleic of more than 3.3 grams per 100 grams. It is intended for refining or for technical purposes.

REFINED OLIVE OIL is olive oil obtained from virgin olive oils by refining methods.

OLIVE OIL or **PURE OLIVE OIL** is oil consisting of a blend of refined olive oil and virgin olive oil.

Finally, there is olive residue oil, which is a crude oil obtained by treating olive residues with solvents, and intended for subsequent refining for human consumption. It is classified as **REFINED OLIVE-RESIDUE OIL**, and is the type used largely in the commercial packaging of foods.

TASTING THE FRUIT OF THE TREE

'**L**'huile qu'on tire ici des plus belles olives du monde remplace le buerre et j'apprehendais bien. Main j'en ai goute dans les sauces et, il n'y a rien meilleur.' RACINE.

Olive oil tastings are becoming popular events. You may be amazed to learn that they even exist! Run by stores, delicatessens and wine shops, they serve the same purpose as a wine tasting, allowing you to sample before buying and to compare different oils. They can be great fun, and are an excellent way for you to discover your personal preferences, before investing in a bottle. Usually there is a supply of bread for you to dip in the oil but if you feel up to it, a sip of oil to swill round the mouth will give the best appreciation, followed by a slice of apple to cleanse the palate. As well as tasting, take a good long sniff — you should be able to detect the fresh, fruity aroma of the olive if it's a good oil.

Not many people have yet had the experience of tasting oils. It is often difficult to find the words to describe different flavours, so the International Olive Oil Council have drawn up a general basic vocabulary for use by their professional tasters, as a way of establishing standards for the organoleptic assessment of virgin olive oils. But this is just as useful for the first-time taster.

GLOSSARY OF TASTING TERMS

ALMOND. This flavour may appear in two forms; that typical of the fresh almond or that peculiar to dried, sound almonds which can be confused with incipient rancidity. A distinctive sensation is perceived as an aftertaste when the oil remains in contact with the tongue and palate. Associated with sweet oils that have a flat odour.

APPLE. Flavour of olive oil which is reminiscent of this fruit.

BITTER. Characteristic taste of oils obtained from green olives, or olives turning colour. It can be more or less pleasant depending on its intensity.

BRINE. Taste of oil extracted from olives which have been preserved in saline solutions.

CUCUMBER. Flavour produced when an oil is hermetically packed for too long, particularly in tin containers.

EARTHY. Characteristic of oil obtained from olives which have been collected with earth or mud on them and not washed. This flavour may sometimes be accompanied by a musty-humid odour.

ESPARTO. Characteristic of oil obtained from olives pressed in new esparto mats. This flavour may differ depending on whether the mats are made of green esparto or dried esparto.

FLAT OR SMOOTH. Olive oil whose organoleptic characteristics are very weak owing to the loss of their aromatic components.

FRUITY. Reminiscent of both the odour and taste of sound fresh fruit picked at its optimum stage of ripeness.

GRASS. Taste reminiscent of recently mown grass.

GREEN LEAVES (BITTER). Flavour of oil obtained from excessively green olives or olives that have been crushed with leaves and twigs.

TABLE OLIVES

In our pursuit to find the best olive oil, we must not forget that the fruit itself offers a myriad of tastes when preserved whole. There are delectable ranges of table olives; green or black, small and hard, large and fleshy, pitted or stuffed with pimento, almonds, anchovy, capers or garlic, packed in brine or loose in oil and aromatics, and cracked in the Greek style — the variety is enormous.

Just to journey through the Mediterranean sampling locally

HARSH. Sensation of certain oils which when tasted produce a reaction of astringency.

HAY. Flavour of certain oils reminiscent of dried grass.

HEATED OR BURNT. Flavour caused by excessive heating during processing, particularly when the paste is thermally mixed, if this is done under unsuitable conditions.

METALLIC. Characteristic of oils which have been in prolonged contact, under unsuitable conditions with foodstuffs or metallic surfaces during crushing, mixing, pressing or storage.

MUSTINESS-HUMIDITY. Flavour of oils obtained from fruit in which large numbers of fungi and yeasts have developed, as a result of the olives being stored in piles for several days.

OLD. Oil that has been kept too long in storage containers, also possibly appearing in oils which have been packed for an excessively long time.

RANCID. The flavour common to all oils and fats that have undergone a process of auto-oxidation caused by prolonged contact with the air. This is an unpleasant taste and cannot be corrected.

RIPELY FRUITY. Taste of oil obtained from ripe fruit, generally having a somewhat flat odour and a sweet taste.

ROUGH. Causing a thick, pasty sensation in the mouth.

SWEET. Pleasant taste, not exactly sugary but found in an oil in which the bitter, astringent and pungent attributes do not predominate.

WINEY-VINEGARY. Flavour of certain oils due mainly to the formation of acetic acid, ethyl acetate and ethanol in larger amounts than is usual in the aroma of olive oil.

prepared olives, would offer the traveller an exquisite organoleptic experience.

When the olives first start to form on the tree they contain no oil, only a mixture of organic acids and sugars By the magic of nature a transformation gradually occurs, as the olive ripens. A chemical process, called lipogenesis, slowly turns the acids and sugars into oil, as the olives turn from palest green through rose and violet to black. Olives can be picked at any stage through the process, and the degree of ripeness will determine its taste.

You will have noticed the difference in taste between a green

A SELECTION OF OLIVE VARIETIES

Olea Europaea

Spring Blossom

Manzanilla   *Niçoise*   *Kalamata*   *Arbequina*

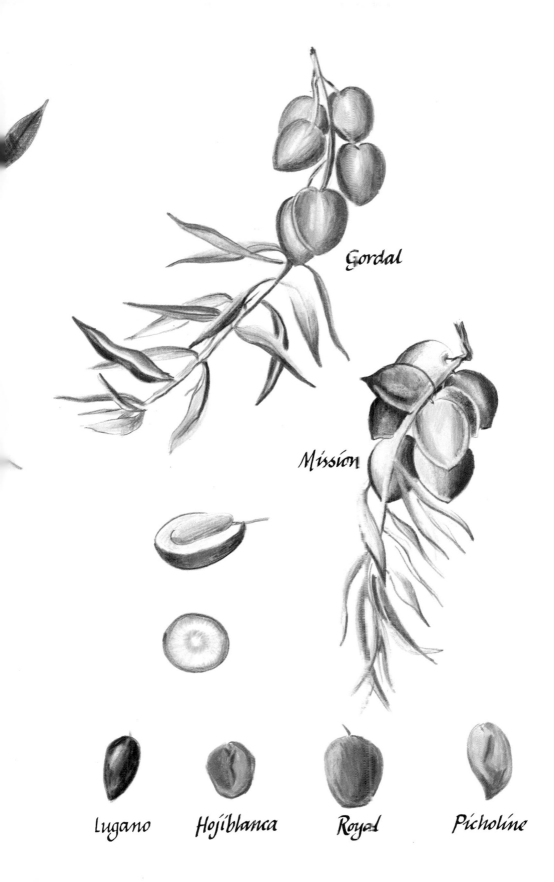

Gordal

Mission

Lugano   Hojiblanca   Royal   Picholine

and a black olive. You may like one but not the other. Green olives have very little oil, their flesh is firm because they aren't yet ripe, and they have a sharp tang. Black olives are full of oil, the flesh is soft because they are ripe and they have a mellower flavour.

Green olives, because they are unripe are inedible, unless treated to remove their bitter glucosides. This is done on a commercial basis by immersing the olives in a soda solution, and then washing them thoroughly in clean water, after which they are packed in brine. During this process the olives must be kept away from the air, to prevent them turning brown through oxidation. For centuries, however, the growers who prepare their own olives have simply washed them every day for about ten days in fresh water and then immersed them in brine, which is often mixed with herbs or lemon or other aromatic ingredients. These combinations of herbs and aromatics can vary from region to region, even from family to family, and there are many secret recipes which have been passed down from generation to generation.

Black olives in contrast, being fully ripe, only need washing and preserving in brine or dry salt.

Most consumers will not be in a position to treat fresh olives from their own trees, but you can buy stoned or unstoned green and black olives, loose or packed in brine and preserve them in a variety of ways yourself.

If you should, however, manage to obtain fresh olives then you simply immerse them in cold water and change the water every day for 10 days. Then make a brine solution using about 500g (1lb) of salt to 5kg (10lb) of olives. You can test to see if the strength of the solution is correct by seeing if an egg will float in it. Leave the olives in this for 3–4 weeks. They are then ready to eat

If you are using black olives, you can dry salt them by mixing equal quantities of olives and salt. Put them in a sack or a container which will allow the juice to flow out, weigh them down and leave for a month.

When green and black olives have been prepared in brine and are ready for eating, you can then preserve them in some of the following ways.

GREEN OLIVES WITH PRESERVED LEMONS

jar of green olives in brine
sliced peel of 1 preserved lemon
   (see recipe on page 135)

sprig of thyme

Drain the olives keeping half the brine. Pack the jar with the olives, lemon peel, and thyme. Mix the brine with enough olive oil and white wine vinegar to fill the jar and pour over the olives. Leave for a couple of weeks.

GARLIC OLIVES

jar of green olives in brine
2 cloves of garlic, crushed

pinch of oregano

Use the same method as before, adding the garlic and oregano.

CRACKED GREEN OLIVES

1kg (2lb) green olives
2–3 cloves of garlic, peeled and
   whole

90ml (6tbs) coriander seeds
60ml (4tbs) oregano
olive oil

Rinse the olives first and then crack them with a hammer to break the flesh. Be careful not to crack the stone. Put a layer of olives in a large, glass jar, sprinkle with some coriander seeds and oregano and a clove of garlic and repeat until you have filled the jar. Top with olive oil so that it completely covers the olives. Leave for 2–3 weeks.

MARINATED BLACK OLIVES

500g (1lb) black olives
30ml (2tbs) red wine vinegar
2 cloves of garlic

15ml (1tsp) paprika
1 slice of lemon
olive oil

Mix together the red wine vinegar, garlic, paprika and lemon. Stir in the black olives. Put into a jar and add enough olive oil to fill it. These will be best after a couple of weeks.

Contrary to long held beliefs that frying with olive oil makes food greasy, it is excellent for use at the high temperature required for deep frying. It has a smoking point of about 210°C, which is higher than for butter (110°C), margarine (150°C), corn oil (160°C), or sunflower and soyabean oil (170°C).

    Olive oil increases in volume on being heated, so it is economical for cooking. It can be used a number of times, providing it is filtered each time after use and is never mixed with new oil. In cooking it is best to use a good measure of oil and pour off the excess, filtering it and storing it out of the light. All olive oil should be stored, away from heat, light and air. As with all other fats and oils, it must never be allowed to smoke when being heated. This is a sign of overheating the oil turns black and forms acrolein, which is a toxin.

You may sometimes see olive oil with a white solid layer at the bottom of the bottle. This happens when it has been exposed to the cold, and will not damage or change the oil in any way. When returned to normal room temperature, the oil becomes liquid again. Its solidification point is 2°C. So don't store olive oil in a fridge.

L'Olivier Shop, Rue de Rivoli, Paris

OLIVE OIL AND HEALTH

'Olive oil makes all your aches and pains go away.'

ANCIENT PROVERB

For centuries the benefits of olive oil nutritionally, cosmetically and medicinally have been recognised by the people of the Mediterranean. In the Bible for instance, its healing powers are amply demonstrated in the famous parable, where the Good Samaritan tends to the robbed man by pouring oil and wine into his wounds.

In Greek and Roman times, people cleaned their skins by rubbing themselves with olive oil, then scraping it off with a curved blade of wood or bronze called a strigil. Housed in the British Museum today, there is a fine example of a bronze pot for holding olive oil with two strigils, as used by Greek athletes. Olive oil was also used to maintain the suppleness of skin and muscle, to heal abrasions and to soothe the burning and drying effects of sun and wind. Women used it especially to give body and shine to their hair. Mixed with spices or herbs, it was administered both internally and externally for health and beauty.

Both Pliny and Hippocrates prescribed medications containing olive oil and olive leaves, as cures for a number of disorders ranging from inflammation of the gums, insomnia, and nausea to boils. Many of these old remedies have passed into folk medicine and are still as relevant today as they were hundreds of years ago.

Byron's description of the Mediterranean as 'where the citron and the olive are the fairest of fruit' was apt. The influence of both is to be found in the cooking of Spain, the South of France, Italy, Greece, Turkey, Morocco, Tunisia, Portugal, Egypt, Jordan, Lebanon and all the islands which are scattered between these shores. The ingredients which go into Mediterranean dishes are the products of unsophisticated, agricultural communities. In this harsh and arid landscape, only hardy and vigorous trees can survive. Nowhere do you find the lush green grass of northern

FOLK REMEDIES USING OLIVE OIL

FOR SHINING HAIR After shampooing rub in a mixture of olive oil and egg yolk, juice of a lemon and a little beer. Leave for 5 minutes and wash out.

TO PREVENT DANDRUFF. Rub into the hair a mixture of olive oil and eau de Cologne. Then rinse.

FOR DRY SKIN. Make a face mask with an avocado and olive oil. Leave for 10 minutes and then rinse off.

TO PREVENT WRINKLES. Rub into the skin a mixture of olive oil and the juice of a lemon before going to bed.

TO SOFTEN THE SKIN. Mix together equal parts of olive oil and salt. Massage the body and wash off.

FOR WEAK NAILS. Soak the nails for 5 minutes in warm olive oil and then paint the nails with white iodine.

FOR TIRED FEET. Massage with olive oil.

FOR ACHING MUSCLES. Massage with a mixture of olive oil and rosemary.

TO CLEAR ACNE. Rub with a mixture of 250ml (8fl oz) olive oil and 10 drops of lavender oil.

TO REDUCE THE EFFECTS OF ALCOHOL. Take a couple of spoonfuls of olive oil before drinking.

FOR HIGH BLOOD PRESSURE. Boil 24 olive leaves in 250ml (8fl oz) of water for 15 minutes. Drink the liquid morning and night for two weeks.

Europe, where cattle can graze, and hence where meat and dairy products are prevalent. What you do find is the olive tree, the vine, lemon and orange trees, wild aromatic herbs, and an abundance of sea food.

Recent research has now provided firm proof that a Mediterranean-style diet, which includes olive oil, is not only generally healthy, but that consuming olive oil can actually reduce cholesterol levels.

The increase in heart disease since the war was an alarming indicator that something in the contemporary industrialized lifestyle was to blame. This led the American Heart Foundation to initiate research into the modern diet, smoking, obesity and high blood pressure. They found that in Greece and especially on the

island of Crete, the mortality rate due to cardiovascular illnesses was the lowest in the world — while Finland and the United States had the highest coronary mortalities. The only variable in the populations studied proved to be the type of fat ingested. In the countries with the highest incidences of cardiovascular diseases, saturated fats are consumed most often and these fats were discovered to cause an increase in cholesterol levels. Monounsaturates, on the other hand, contain no cholesterol. Over the last twenty years a number of medical congresses, promoted by the International Olive Oil Council, have studied the role of fats in the human diet. These have revealed what an important role olive oil has to play in maintaining good health.

Fats or lipids are essential in a well balanced diet. They divide

into saturates and unsaturates, depending on whether they have simple or double bonds between their carbon groups. Fatty acids that have one double bond are monounsaturates. Polyunsaturates have several double bonds. Olive oil and other vegetable oils contain unsaturated fatty acids. Oleic acid and linoleic acid are two unsaturated fatty acids. Olive oil is 80% oleic acid, placing it at the top of the list of monounsaturated fats. The two main polyunsaturated fatty acids are linoleic and linolenic acid, and these are found in large quantities in sunflower and corn oils. Saturated fatty acids, on the other hand, are found in animal fats, such as butter and lard.

COMPOSITION of OLIVE OIL

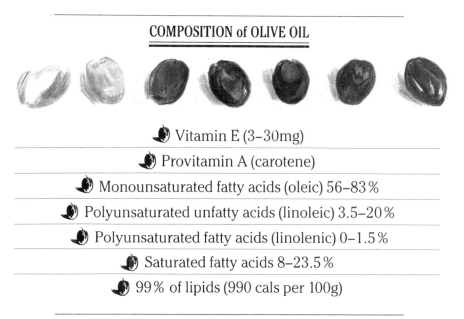

- Vitamin E (3–30mg)
- Provitamin A (carotene)
- Monounsaturated fatty acids (oleic) 56–83%
- Polyunsaturated unfatty acids (linoleic) 3.5–20%
- Polyunsaturated fatty acids (linolenic) 0–1.5%
- Saturated fatty acids 8–23.5%
- 99% of lipids (990 cals per 100g)

Low fat diets have long been recommended to reduce cholesterol. This meant cutting down on the intake of animal fats and using polyunsaturated fats in the form of vegetable oil.

Polyunsaturated fats have been heavily promoted over the last few years as the answer to a balanced fat intake, but in 1986 the results of research into monounsaturated fatty acids came up with some startling new evidence about the nature of cholesterol. There are two types, low density (LDL) and high density (HDL). Low density lipoproteins (LDL) transport and deposit cholesterol in the tissues and arteries. LDL increases with a high intake of saturated fatty acids and is therefore harmful, because it will deposit more cholesterol. High density lipoproteins (HDL) eliminate cholesterol from the cells, and carry it to the liver where it is passed out through the bile ducts. While polyunsaturates reduce both LDL and HDL, monounsaturates reduce LDL while increasing HDL. An increase in the level of HDL will not only provide protection against cholesterol deposits, but it will actually reduce cholesterol levels in the body.

All this evidence has been supported by numbers of studies conducted in Spain and the USA. Volunteers were put on diets using only olive oil, and then compared to another group who used only sunflower seed oil. The research showed that those using olive oil significantly increased their levels of HDL. Olive oil as the main source of monounsaturated fatty acids has to be the best form of fat to use.

The healthy aspects of olive oil are not only limited to its efficacy with regard to the heart. Research has also taken place over the years into its many other positive benefits on the human body.

The oil, taken heated or unheated, has been shown to reduce gastric acidity, and its emollient effect protects against ulcers and aids the passage of food through the intestines. In other words, it helps prevent constipation.

It stimulates bile secretion and provokes contraction of the gall-bladder, reducing the risk of gallstones. Since olive oil contains Vitamin E and oleic acid, which is also found in human milk, it aids normal bone growth and is most suitable for both expectant and nursing mothers because it encourages development of the infant's brain and nervous system before and after birth.

Finally, as if this combination of attributes was not enough, olive oil has also been shown to prevent the wear and tear of age on the functioning of the brain and on the ageing of the tissues and organs in general.

All this mountain of evidence proves conclusively that olive oil, of all the fats available, is highly beneficial to you whatever your age or lifestyle.

SPAIN

L ast December, just before Christmas, I drove almost the entire length of Spain starting in the cold, grey north and finishing in the unseasonable warmth and Moorish magnificence of the south. I was visiting producers and witnessing the olive harvest in full swing. The more I go to Spain, the more I love the country and its people. Going back there on my particular mission took me off the beaten track and into tiny villages, nestled in

rugged countryside, that I would on other occasions have rushed past, without a backward glance.

I must confess that I caused much friendly mirth whenever I stopped to chat to the pickers. They watched me wading ankle deep through the muddy groves in shoes instead of rubber boots, which by the time I had reached them in the middle of the field, looked like a pair of brown flippers!

I most enjoy visiting countries out of season, when the tourists have gone and places return to their normal, relaxed pace. There was no denying that Spain in December was different. The towns were decked out with Christmas lights and silken banners declaring 'Feliz Navidad'. In Barcelona I discovered a tiny market only selling Christmas trees, decorations and all the paraphernalia for making cribs. The air had the delicious sweet smell of pine and everyone was in high spirits.

I had selected Spain for my first foray because it is the world's largest producer of olive oil. This may come as a surprise to many people who assume that Italy tops the league table. In fact Italy comes a close second with Greece, Turkey and Tunisia following behind.

The great revelation when you start discovering the world of the olive is that each country produces olive oils of vastly differing flavours, and within each country every region produces an olive oil different from the oil produced a few miles away, even when the same variety of olive is being grown. This is because the soils and the microclimates are different and, as with grapes, these factors affect the taste of the fruit.

Anyone who has been to Spain but who hasn't travelled inland may be amazed to learn that Spain has over 190 million olive trees, more than anywhere else in the world!

As the world's leading producer, she exported, in 1986, to Europe and the USA, just under 100,000 tonnes of olives. Incidentally, only 1000 tonnes were exported to Britain compared to 50,000 tonnes to the USA.

Sadly most people haven't yet sampled the wonderful extra virgin olive oils the Spanish are producing, unless while on holiday. In fact, some people may still be under the total misapprehension, that it was olive oil which caused many deaths in the oil scandal in Spain in 1981. It was actually toxic rape seed oil – so you need have no fears whatsoever about the purity of Spanish olive oil.

If you have not yet tasted Spanish olive oil, then you will be very agreeably surprised. Go out tomorrow and buy a bottle of extra virgin, sample it and you will realise that it is very different to the Italian and French olive oils which you may have been using.

The olive was probably introduced to Spain by the Carthaginians in the 4th century BC, when they controlled much of the Iberian peninsula. Its growth flourished to such an extent that the Romans, during their occupation, exported vast quantities of Spanish olive oil back to Rome. How indeed history turns full circle, because today, Spain's major export market is Italy as the Italians do not produce sufficient olive oil for their domestic consumption. In 1987, Spain exported over 62 million litres of olive oil, 850,000 litres came to the UK but the USA imported 6 million litres.

Archaeological evidence has shown the magnitude of Roman exports of Spanish olive oil. In 1878, Heinrich Dressel, an archaeologist, was excavating on Mount Testaccio, on the banks of the Tiber in Rome and discovered that the 30-metre high wall consisted of 40 million broken amphorae, the majority of which had come from Spain. Their inscriptions bore the word *Betica*, the Roman name for Spain and they had been used to transport olive oil to Rome. The capacity of each amphora was calculated to have been 50 litres. In fact, shards of such amphorae have been found all over Europe indicating the extent of production in Spain under Roman rule.

It is interesting, however, that the Spanish word for oil is *aceite*, which derives from the Arabic and not as you might expect from the Latin of the Romans. This is a legacy from the 700 years of rule by the Moors, who brought with them citrus fruits and spices as well as the magnificent architectural styles seen in the great Andalusian cities of Seville, Cordoba and Granada.

Spain was the first country in Europe to establish a Denominacion de Origen (officially demarcated producing areas) for olive oils, in the same way they exist for wine.

The Spanish Denominacion de Origen only applies to virgin olive oils. This is because these are the only grades of olive oils which conserve in their production methods, the natural attributes derived from their environment, from the olives used, and from cultural factors specific to the region concerned, such as form and timing of harvesting. The rigorous controls of the DO, which we all expect in wines, are proof of how highly the Spanish regard their olive oil.

There are currently four demarcated areas in Spain, two authorized and two which are provisional — these are Borjas Blancas, Siurana, Sierra de Segura and Baena.

Borjas Blancas was the first olive oil granted a label of origin. This area consists of a collection of towns clustered together in the south of the province of Lerida, in the Las Garrigas and La Segarra Baja districts, in southern Catalonia. Its countryside, neither very beautiful nor dramatic, consists of small hills and narrow lowland

Borjas Blancas

valleys. In the summer there are long periods of drought but the olive is perfectly adapted to this environment, producing small but very high quality crops of olives.

The harvesting technique in this region is known as 'milking', which is manual collection, bough by bough. Olive groves cover 35,000 hectares and produce an average of 5,000 metric tonnes of olive oil per year. The Arbequina olive variety, rich in oil, is the most common in Borjas Blancas, followed by the Verdiell. Olive oils made under the DO regulations must contain at least 90% of oil from the Arbequina variety.

Two types of oil are made depending on the time at which the olives are harvested. There is a fruity green oil made from early picked olives, full bodied with a bitter, almond taste. Then there is a sweet, yellow oil made from olives harvested later. Most of the production of this area is exported, Italy being the principal customer.

One of the most delicious olive oils available in the shops from this region is Lerida. Packaged in a beautiful glass decanter, it has a cork stopper and red wax to seal in its potent aroma. The Vea family estate is just outside the tiny village of Sarroca de Lerida and has been producing high quality extra virgin for three generations. When I visited, I was shown family photographs of the ancient wooden lever press which was used until they went over to modern computerised machinery. They harvest, solely by hand, organically grown Arbequina olives. The trees are never sprayed with pesticides or insecticides. The Vea family take great pride in the clarity of their olive oil so before bottling, it is filtered through natural vegetable papers. The Veas, like so many other producers in Spain, have tankers leaving every week from outside the low, whitewashed, stone warehouse, destined for Italy. They also export to the Japanese, who are now one of the most enthusiastic and knowledgeable markets, the United States, Canada, Australia and New Zealand as well as the rest of the EEC.

Siuarana is the second DO and comprises a wide band of country which crosses the Catalonian province of Tarragona from west to east. Within the DO there are two clearly defined districts; the first, further inland is in the foothills of the Sierra Montsant mountains. Hilly, rugged land — and difficut to cultivate. Nearer the coast lies the Campo de Tarragona, a much smoother terrain with soils of better composition. This DO has around 10,000 hectares of olive groves and produces about 2,100 metric tonnes of oil per year. The oil from this area is made exclusively from the Arbequina, Rojal and Morrut (Morruda) varieties and has a fine aroma. As with Borjas Blancas, there are two types of oil depending on the ripeness of the olives.

Sierra de Segura has a provincial DO. The olive-growing area is in the north-east of the province of Jaen in Andalucia and covers 38,000 hectares of rugged terrain with steep slopes which makes mechanisation difficult, so the olives have to be harvested by hand.

The virgin oils of this district are fruity, aromatic and slightly bitter and are mostly made from the Picual olve. This region is truly the heart of Spanish olive growing; I drove for hours round Jaen and saw nothing but rows of olive trees stretching to the horizon. In the early morning during the harvest, landrovers and cars packed inside with pickers and outside with nets and poles headed out of tiny hamlets, towards the fields. In the evenings the processions return, while tractors bearing the day's load of olives, make for the local mill. At dusk the drivers stand around patiently smoking and chatting while they wait their turn to drive in, and

Seville

have their cargo carefully weighed and pressed.

The production area of Baena is also provisional, and it extends along the south of the province of Cordoba, between the lowlands and the areas neighbouring the Penibetic mountains. Groves of Picudo, Carrasquena, Picual, Hojiblanca and Lechin olives mantle 32,000 hectares. The oils from this DO are yellow, with a green and violet tinge and the flavours vary between intense and fruity, and smooth and sweet.

In Spain, as in all the olive-growing countries, there are thousands of small growers who take their olives to the local co-operative where the olives are milled and pressed. The virgin oil produced may then be purchased, bottled and marketed internationally by large distributors such as Ybarra, in Seville and Carbonell, near Cordoba in the heart of Andalusia who have been producing olive oil since 1866. Carbonell's bottles of oil carry the distinctive and charming picture of a Spanish lady wrapped in a red shawl plucking an olive from a tree.

Extra virgin oils from these companies are excellent, which is not surprising. Because of their size they have the choice of the finest virgin oils in the region. Tankers from local co-operatives deliver to the Carbonell and Ybarra factories, samples are immediately taken from the consignment and then rushed to the laboratory where they are tested for acidity before being accepted. If accepted, the virgin oil may be bottled as extra virgin, depending on the acidity, or added to refined oil and sold as pure olive oil.

As well as being the major producer of olive oil, Spain is justly famous for its table olives, most of which come from Andalusia. The best known of the varieties is the Manzanilla. Picked when green, this is the one you are most likely to buy under the general label 'Spanish olives'. The Gordal or Queen as it's also known, the largest and most fleshy of the Spanish olives, is picked both when green and black. Hojiblanca is less highly regarded, but it is a hardy, large cropping variety, and is used for oil as well as being preserved. Then there are Blanguetas, most often marketed at pink-brown ripeness, for eating.

Many of the olives are sold stuffed with pimiento, almonds, onion or garlic. In days gone by these were stoned and stuffed by hand — a labour intensive job if ever there was one — but today the inevitable machines grade the table olives according to their size, stone them and stuff them at the same rate of 2000 per minute; what used to take 20 women 8 hours, can now be done in 1 hour by machine.

Recipes using olives and olive oil abound in Spanish cooking. Olive oil is used for frying fish and meat as well as sweet dishes like Churros — deep-fried strips of batter coated in sugar, which the Spanish eat in the morning with hot chocolate or coffee.

It is also used in making dough for tortas and empanadas, and numerous different types of bread. It is added raw as a condiment to improve the texture, taste and nutritive values of dishes such as Gazpacho — and, of course, it appears in green salads and in dishes like hervido, which contains boiled potatoes, courgettes and aubergine, tossed in oil, like a hot salad. Throughout Spain olive oil preserves cheeses, sausages, fish or vegetables, often with the addition of spices or herbs.

Spanish cooking is still unfortunately much under-rated, perhaps because Spanish restaurants abroad are still a rarity. I am happy to report that now there are, however, tapas bars springing up in the UK and USA. The name comes from the days when a small plate or tapa was placed on a glass of wine or beer to keep out the dust and flies. Then no doubt, one day long ago, an enterprising bar owner popped a couple of olives or anchovies onto the plate as an appetiser and one of the most delightful Spanish traditions was born.

Spain used to be a very poor country but today in cities such as Madrid, you witness sophistication and wealth — a stylish younger generation confidently parading its designer labels on the wide elegant streets. Suddenly Spain is drawing the attention of the rest of the world; all things Spanish are now very much in vogue and it could be that the day for Spanish cuisine has also finally come.

AJO BLANCHO DE ALMENDRAS
(WHITE GARLIC SOUP)

A soup made of bread, almonds, oil, garlic and water may sound an unlikely combination but to my mind this is one of the most delicious dishes to serve as a summer starter. Friends who have tasted this have all marvelled at the ingredients and have usually asked for second helpings. This is a typical Spanish dish dating back to Roman times, when it was known as 'what a mess', which meant it contained everything barring the kitchen sink! Usually garnished with white grapes, this version which has raisins and diced apple, was served to me in the El Caballo Rojo restaurant in Cordoba and it is the best I have tasted.

To serve 4

4 slices stale white bread, without
  crusts
cold water
4 cloves of garlic
1 cup almonds, blanched and
  peeled
4tbs olive oil
3tbs white wine vinegar, ideally
  sherry vinegar

salt, to taste

FOR GARNISH
1 eating apple,
  diced
raisins

Soak the bread in water and squeeze dry. Put the salt and the peeled cloves of garlic in a mortar or food processor and grind thoroughly. Add the almonds little by little until everything is mixed to a paste. Add the bread, then start adding a dash of oil drop by drop until you have the consistency of mayonnaise. Add the vinegar drop by drop, beating the whole time. Add enough cold water to obtain a thick beverage. Add more salt and vinegar if necessary. You may sieve the mixture at this point if you wish but I think it is better left unsieved. Chill the soup and just before serving add the diced apple and raisins. You can use washed white grapes instead of the apple and raisins.

NB *The proportions of garlic, olive oil and vinegar you use depend entirely on your preference, so taste all the time while you are making this soup.*

Olive oil being served as an accompaniment to soup

GAZPACHO

There are many versions of this classic Spanish soup, which originated in Andalusia. The recipes can vary from town to town but the basic ingredients are tomatoes and bread, and in fact gazpacho is supposed to derive from the Arabic word for 'soaked bread'. It traditionally comes with a variety of garnishes, such as cucumbers, croutons, hard boiled eggs, chopped olives and onions, served in little bowls on the table, to be sprinkled on the soup before serving. Most recipes use red or white wine vinegar but I like to use sherry vinegar for added piquancy. How you season the soup will depend on how sweet the tomatoes are.

To serve 4–6

3 slices of bread, without crusts
1¼ cups canned tomato juice
1lb 10oz tomatoes, blanched,
   peeled and chopped
1 green pepper, seeded and
   chopped
1 red pepper, seeded and chopped
½ cucumber, peeled and chopped
3 cloves of garlic
3–5tbs red, white or sherry
   vinegar

6tbs olive oil
salt and pepper, to taste

FOR GARNISH
½ cucumber, peeled and diced
small croutons
hard boiled eggs, diced
1 onion, finely diced
green or black olives, chopped

Soak the bread in the tomato juice for a few minutes then squeeze the bread reserving the juice. In a large bowl mix the bread, garlic, peppers, cucumber and tomatoes. Puree the mixture in batches in a blender or processor to a smooth paste. Stir in the reserved tomato juice. Add the vinegar, olive oil and salt and pepper. If the mixture is too thick you can thin it with cold water. Chill the soup for a couple of hours. You can add a handful of ice cubes before serving if you wish. Serve with bowls of garnishes.

CHAMPINONES AL AJILLO
(MUSHROOMS IN GARLIC)

 The Spaniards eat their evening meal late, usually after nine o'clock, so the early evening occupation is to stroll from bar to bar, enjoying a glass of fino and nibbling tapas. This tasty tapas recipe from Alicia Rios can be served with drinks before a meal or as part of a mixed hors d'oeuvre.

To serve 4, as a starter, more if served as tapas

1lb mushrooms	1tbs chopped parsley
6tbs olive oil	juice of $\frac{1}{2}$ lemon
3 cloves of garlic, finely sliced	salt, to taste
1 or 2 chilli peppers	

Wash the mushrooms and depending on their size slice them or leave them whole, trimming the ends off the stalks. Heat the olive oil, add the garlic and chilli peppers. Before they start to brown, add the mushrooms, season with salt and saute over a strong flame. Turn down the heat and stir in the lemon juice and the parsley. Saute until the juices from the mushrooms have evaporated. Remove the mushrooms from the pan and serve immediately.

ESCABECHE DE CONEJO
(MARINATED RABBIT)

 This is another dish which can be served as a tapas. It is also ideal served on a large platter as a snack at a drinks party, with cocktail sticks for the guests to spear the morsels of meat. I first tasted this at the party to celebrate the opening of the Oxford branch of Books for Cooks, and was so taken with it, that Alicia Rios kindly gave me the recipe. You can substitute chicken or turkey for the rabbit.

To serve between 10 and 20 people, depending on how hungry they are

1½lb rabbit
1 medium onion
4 cloves
1 head of garlic
1 carrot, cut in two
5ml (1tsp) peppercorns
3 sprigs of thyme

1 bay leaf
1 cup olive oil
½ cup sherry vinegar or
  1 cup wine vinegar
1 cup stock or white wine
salt, to taste

Push the cloves into the onion and peel the garlic. Put all the ingredients into a large casserole, put the lid on and cook over a low heat for 1–1½ hours. Leave to marinate for at least three days before eating.

GAMBAS EN SALSA DE ACEITUNAS Y TOMATE
(PRAWNS IN OLIVE AND TOMATO SAUCE)

Many of Spain's most famous dishes use fish and shellfish; even inland fresh seafood, such as clams, lobsters, mussels, scallops, crabs, oysters, crayfish, and prawns are always available. This dish makes a perfect starter.

To serve 4

1 onion, peeled
2 carrots, peeled and sliced
2 sticks of celery, sliced
2tsp ground cumin
2tsp ground ginger
1 small red chilli pepper, thinly
  sliced
2tbs olive oil

2tbs flour
2½ cups fish stock
24 prawns
1lb tomatoes, quartered
1tbs tomato puree
½ cup black olives, stoned
1tbs fresh dill, chopped
salt and pepper, to taste

Fry the onion, carrot, celery, and spices in the olive oil for a few minutes. Stir in the flour and cook for a minute. Gradually stir in the stock and bring to the boil. Remove the shells from the prawns; add the heads and shells to the sauce together with the tomatoes, tomato puree and salt and pepper to taste. Simmer for

about 30 minutes until the sauce has reduced by a quarter. Sieve the sauce and measure off 2 cups. Leave to cool. Halve most of the olives and arrange in a shallow serving dish with the peeled prawns, spoon over the sauce. Cover and chill overnight. When ready to serve, sprinkle with chopped dill, and garnish with the remaining olives.

CANAPE DE PASTA DE ACEITUNA
(GREEN OLIVE PASTE CANAPE)

 A mixture of typical Spanish produce which can be used as a spread on bread to serve as a tapas. An ideal snack to hand round to your guests when you are having a barbeque.

To serve up to 12, as nibbles

40 green olives, stoned
1tsp capers
4 anchovies
1tsp ground almonds
1 clove of garlic

4tbs olive oil
$\frac{1}{4}$tsp ground cumin
$\frac{1}{4}$tsp paprika
$\frac{1}{4}$inch slices of french bread
pimiento for garnish

Place all the ingredients except the bread and pimiento, into a food processor and mix until you have a fine paste. Spread thinly on the slices of bread and decorate with pieces of pimiento.

ENSALADA DE NARANJAS, ACEITUNAS Y JEREZ

(ORANGE, OLIVE AND SHERRY SALAD)

There is a dazzling array of fruit grown in Spain. The market stalls all over the country display kaleidoscopic arrangements of figs, melons, lemons, grapes, apples, dates, strawberries and of course oranges, which are used in this refreshing salad.

To serve 4

4 large oranges
½ cup olive oil
¼ cup dry sherry
1tbs fresh mint, chopped
⅓ cup black olives

3tbs raisins
salt and pepper, to taste

FOR GARNISH
sprigs of fresh mint

Thinly pare the rind from one orange and cut the peel into matchstick strips. Squeeze the juice from the orange. Mix the olive oil with the orange juice, sherry, strips of orange peel, mint, salt and pepper. Peel the remaining oranges and cut into slices. Arrange the orange slices in overlapping rings on a serving dish. Scatter the olives and raisins over the oranges and spoon over about ⅔ of the dressing. Cover and chill for about 2 hours. Just before serving spoon over the remaining dressing and garnish with the sprigs of mint.

ALL-I-OLI
(CATALAN OLIVE OIL AND GARLIC SAUCE)

 This classic Catalan sauce is not a mayonnaise because it does not contain eggs, just olive oil and garlic which makes it a tricky sauce to make since it has a tendency to separate. The answer is to add a small quantity of white crustless bread if it will not thicken. The number of cloves of garlic used will depend on your personal taste and you can add lemon juice if you wish. It is traditionally served with grilled meat or fish or mixed with Romesco.

Makes 1 cup

6–10 cloves of garlic, peeled   salt, to taste
1 cup olive oil

Put the cloves of garlic in a blender with the salt and blend at high speed. With the motor running add the olive oil very slowly until the sauce begins to thicken. If it remains oily add the bread.

ROMESCO

 Catalonian cooking is an assimilation of many influences including French and Italian and as such, sauces form the basis of many dishes. Romesco is the great Catalan sauce. It takes its name from the hot red romesco peppers which grow in this region. The fieriness of the sauce can vary from the tolerable to the explosive, so if you come across it being served in Spain, treat it with respect. In Catalonia, Romesco is often served with a bowl of ali-oli and the two are mixed to taste at the table. The real romesco peppers, which may prove difficult to find outside Spain, can be substituted with chilli peppers but, of course, the taste will not be authentic. The sauce is used to accompany shellfish, fish, meat, poultry as well as stews and salads.

To make about $1\frac{1}{4}$ cups

$\frac{1}{2}$ cup blanched almonds
3 cloves of garlic, unpeeled
2 tomatoes, whole
1 dried romesco pepper or 1 dried
   hot chilli pepper

$\frac{2}{3}$ cup olive oil
3tbs red wine vinegar
salt, to taste

Preheat the oven to 180°C (350°F), Gas Mark 4. Place almonds, garlic, tomatoes and pepper on a baking tray and put in the oven for 10–15 minutes, removing the almonds when they are lightly browned and the tomatoes and garlic when they are soft. Peel the tomatoes and remove the seeds, peel the garlic. Place the tomatoes, garlic, pepper and almonds in a blender and grind thoroughly. Add the vinegar and salt and then gradually blend in the oil, until the mixture thickens.

SALSA DE ACEITUNAS
(GREEN OLIVE SAUCE)

 A simple and quick sauce which can be served with grilled meat or fish or also over pasta.

Makes about $1\frac{1}{4}$ cups

$\frac{2}{3}$ cup green olives, stoned
1 small onion, peeled and sliced
2 cloves of garlic, peeled
2 tomatoes, peeled, seeded and
   chopped

$\frac{1}{4}$ cup white wine or sherry
1 tbs lemon juice
3 tbs olive oil
$\frac{1}{2}$ cup water
salt and pepper, to taste

Place the olives, onion, garlic, tomatoes, wine and lemon juice in a food processor and blend until smooth. Add the olive oil slowly and salt and pepper if necessary. Put the mixture into a saucepan with the water and simmer for 10 minutes.

Early evening tapas in a Spanish bar

Jaen, Andalucía

SALSA DE MOJO

This piquant sauce is unique to the Canary Islands. I have included this recipe because it is often part of tapas, when traditionally served with papas arrugadas — potatoes boiled in their skins with a little water and coarse salt which forms a crust on the potatoes as the water evaporates. But the sauce can also be served with meat or fish.

2–3 large cloves of garlic
1tsp cumin seed
1tsp paprika
pinch of thyme

$\frac{1}{4}$ cup olive oil
2tsp wine vinegar
$\frac{1}{4}$ cup warm water

Peel the garlic and crush in a mortar or in a food processor with the cumin seed. It should be ground very finely. Add the paprika and thyme, then add the olive oil a drop at a time. Add the vinegar, then the water and allow to cool before serving.

TORTILLA DE ACEITUNAS Y PIMENTOS
(PEPPER AND OLIVE TORTILLA)

An omelette, or tortilla as it is known in Spain, is rather thicker and fuller than the traditional French variety. It is delicious when served cold in wedges, as it often is in bars as a tapas. This recipe is wonderful when served hot with its melting cheese topping but it could equally well form part of a cold summer picnic.

To serve 4–6

3tbs olive oil
1 red pepper, pith and seeds
   removed and cut into squares
1 green pepper, pith and seeds
   removed and cut into squares
1 yellow pepper, pith and seeds
   removed and cut into squares

$\frac{1}{4}$ cup green stuffed olives
$\frac{1}{4}$ cup black olives, stoned
6 eggs
2 egg yolks
3oz hard cheese, sliced
salt and pepper, to taste

Heat the oil in a deep pan. Add the peppers and saute gently for 5 minutes, then add the olives and continue cooking for a further 2 minutes. Beat the eggs with the egg yolks and add salt and pepper to taste. Pour into a pan. Cook over a moderate heat until nearly set. Arrange the slices of cheese over the top of the eggs and place under a hot grill for a few minutes until the cheese begins to melt and brown. Slide the tortilla onto a plate and serve cut into wedges with a salad.

DELICIAS DE ARROZ
(SPICY RICE DELICACIES)

 Paella is the best known rice dish from Spain Many people seem to think it is the only dish from Spain! This is a simple variation which includes seafood and olives.

To serve 4

2 cloves of garlic, crushed
½ cup paprika
2tbs olive oil
½ cup diced chicken
1 green pepper, pith and seeds
   removed, sliced
2 large tomatoes, peeled, seeded
   and chopped
¾ cup rice

2½ cups chicken stock
1 sprig of thyme
½tsp saffron
2tsp tomato puree
½ cup prawns peeled
¼ cup stuffed olives, halved
salt and pepper, to taste

Saute the garlic and paprika in the olive oil for a few minutes, add the chicken and cook for a further 3–4 minutes until the chicken is browned. Add the pepper and tomato, and continue cooking for a further 3–4 minutes. Stir in the rice until coated in the oil. Add the stock and bring slowly to the boil. Add the thyme, saffron, tomato puree and salt and pepper to taste. Cover and simmer gently for 20 minutes, If the rice starts to dry out add some water. Stir in the prawns and the olives and continue to simmer until the rice is tender. Serve immediately.

CARNE EN SALSA DE ESPINACAS Y AJOS

(BEEF IN GARLIC AND SPINACH SAUCE)

Jars of black olive pate are widely available now in good food shops and are very useful to keep in the store cupboard. This pate can be used to spread on toast or canapes, and it is also marvellous for a quick sauce for pasta. Here it is used in a sauce for beef.

To serve 4–6

2lb piece topside of beef
2tbs olive oil
6–8 small button onions, peeled
1tbs red wine vinegar
1tbs flour
6oz fresh spinach, washed and
   trimmed

3 cloves of garlic
2½ cups beef stock
salt and pepper, to taste
1tbs black olive pate

In a large casserole, heat the olive oil and brown the beef on all sides and remove. Add the button onions to the pan and stir them round until evenly browned. Pour in the vinegar and simmer briskly for 1 minute. Stir in the flour and cook for a minute. Put the spinach, garlic and half the stock into a

liquidiser and blend until smooth. Add the mixture to the pan together with the remaining stock, salt and pepper. Return the beef to the pan and baste with the sauce. Cover and simmer for about 45 minutes or until the beef is done to your taste. Stir in the black olive pate a few minutes before the end of the cooking time. Slice the beef onto a warm serving dish, pour over the sauce, and serve immediately.

CARNE MACHADA A LA ANDALUZA
(BEEF WITH ALMONDS AND OLIVES)

Almonds often appear in Spanish dishes both sweet and savoury. In this recipe both almonds and olives are mixed and used as a stuffing. An unusual combination perhaps, but a delicious one nonetheless, using two of Andalusia's main crops

To serve 4

2lb lean beef in one piece
1 cup blanched almonds
⅔ cup stoned green olives
5ml (1tsp) cinnamon
olive oil
1 onion, sliced

1 tomato, peeled and chopped
1 clove of garlic, peeled
¾ cup red wine
1¼ cup stock
salt and pepper, to taste

Make deep cuts in the beef and fill them with a mixture of chopped almonds, chopped olives, salt and cinnamon. Tie up the meat and brown it in olive oil in a casserole. When the meat is brown all over, add the tomato, onion, and garlic. Add the glass of wine and the stock. Season, cover the casserole and cook on a very low flame until the meat is tender, about 2–3 hours. Remove the beef and slice it onto a warm serving dish, and strain the sauce over it.

BRAZO DE GITANO DE CARNE Y ACEITUNAS
(OLIVE ROMANY)

 The Spanish omelette is famous the world over. In this recipe a small plain omelette is combined with olives, to make an unusual stuffing for beef. This is an age old family recipe from Marie Jose Sevilla, of Foods from Spain.

3 eggs	½tsp thyme
1¼ lb skirt of beef	½ cup dry white wine
⅔ cup stoned green olives	1 cup beef stock
1½tbs flour	salt and pepper, to taste
4tbs olive oil	

Using the eggs make three small plain omelettes. Lay the skirt of beef flat and using a sharp knife, cut a layer across the meat to within 1″ of the opposite side. Roll back the top layer and season with salt and pepper. Place the omelettes and olives on top of the meat covering the whole surface. Roll the meat up, secure with string and dust it with flour. Heat the olive oil and brown the meat. Add the thyme and the wine and cook for a few minutes. Reduce the heat, add the stock and simmer for about an hour or until the meat is tender, adding more stock if necessary. When the meat is tender place it on a large serving dish and remove the string. Allow the meat to rest for a few minutes and then slice it. Pour the juices from the pan over the beef and serve immediately.

POLLO A LA CHILINDRON
(CHICKEN WITH PEPPERS, TOMATOES AND OLIVES)

 This is a dish from the Aragon region of north east Spain, where sauces are a speciality. Many meat dishes are prepared with this sharp, fresh tasting chilindron sauce, so you can use lamb or pork instead of the chicken.

To serve 4–6

4lb chicken, cut into serving
   pieces
$\frac{1}{4}$ cup olive oil
2 cloves of garlic, finely chopped
1 large onion, sliced
3 small red or green peppers, pith
   and seeds removed, sliced
$\frac{1}{3}$ cup finely chopped smoked ham

1lb medium tomatoes, peeled,
   seeded and finely chopped
6 black olives, stoned and halved
6 green olives, stoned and halved
salt and pepper, to taste

Season the chicken pieces with salt and pepper. Heat the olive oil in a large
pan and fry the chopped garlic. Brown the chicken in the oil and remove.
Add the onion, peppers and ham to the pan and cook over a moderate heat
for a few minutes, then add the tomatoes and bring to the boil. Return the
chicken to the pan, cover and simmer gently until the chicken is cooked.
Stir in the olives and serve at once.

POLLO AL JEREZ
(CHICKEN WITH SHERRY)

 Jerez de la Frontera in southern Spain is the 'home' of Sherry, our
English word being a corruption of Jerez and this dish combining
olives and sherry is pure Andalusian.

To serve 4

1 chicken, about 4lb, cut into
   serving pieces
2 onions, chopped
3 cloves of garlic, crushed
2 bay leaves
1tsp oregano

$\frac{1}{2}$tsp chilli powder
24 green olives
$1\frac{1}{2}$ cups of dry sherry
a little cornflour
salt, to taste

Cover the chicken with boiling water and simmer for 15 minutes. Add the
onion, garlic, bay leaves, oregano and salt and cook for a further 30
minutes. Just before the chicken is cooked add the chilli powder, olives and
sherry and simmer for 5 minutes or until the chicken is tender. Remove the
chicken to a serving plate and if necessary thicken the sauce with the
cornflour mixed with a little cold water and cook for a further 5 minutes.
Pour the sauce over the chicken and serve with plain boiled rice.

SALMONETES ANDALUZA
(RED MULLET, ANDALUSIAN STYLE)

 The extensive coastline of Spain teems with a wonderful variety of every kind of fish and shellfish, and not surprisingly they form an important part of the Spanish diet. The red mullets in this recipe are marinated in a mixture of olive oil, garlic and pine nuts before being cooked.

To serve 4

4 red mullet, cleaned, with eyes
  removed
1 cup pine nuts, ground
2 cloves garlic, crushed
1 onion, finely diced
4tbs chopped parsley
½ cup olive oil

juice of 1 lemon
1 green pepper, pith and seeds
  removed, sliced
4 tomatoes, peeled, seeded and
  chopped
4 black olives

Combine the pine nuts, garlic, onion, parsley and lemon juice, and gradually beat in the olive oil. Put the red mullet in a large shallow dish and pour over the marinade. Set aside at room temperature for an hour. Preheat the oven to 180° (350°F), Gas Mark 4. Arrange the slices of pepper over the fish and cover with the tomatoes. Drizzle a little more olive oil over the tomatoes and bake for 35 minutes or until the fish is cooked. Arrange the fish on a warmed serving dish and place the olives in the uppermost eye socket of each fish. Serve immediately.

BONITO CON ACEITUNAS
(TUNA WITH OLIVES)

 Andalusia is renowned throughout Spain for the lightness of its fried food especially fried fish. In such a hot climate there is no place for heavy dishes and this recipe, is typical of the simple but imaginative way much Andalusian food is prepared.

To serve 4

4 tuna steaks
⅔ cup olive oil
¾ cup white wine
1tsp wine vinegar
2 cloves of garlic, peeled and
   crushed

1 bay leaf
sprig of thyme
flour
⅔ cup stoned green olives,
   chopped
salt and pepper, to taste

Place tuna steaks in a shallow dish. Make the marinade with the olive oil, wine, vinegar, herbs, garlic and salt and pour over the fish. Leave to stand in a cool place for at least 2 hours. Remove the fish from the marinade, pat dry and dip into the flour, shaking off the excess. Heat some olive oil in a deep pan and fry the steaks until golden on both sides and the flesh is tender. Remove and keep warm. In the same pan add the marinade and boil until it has reduced a little. Strain it through a sieve, add the chopped olives and pour over the fish.

CHURROS
(FRIED PASTRIES)

 Churros are fluted, sausage-shaped, deep-fried fritters which the Spanish eat warm, dusted with sugar, dipped into their milky coffee or chocolate, for breakfast and through the morning.

To serve 4

2 cups water
½tsp salt
2 cups flour, sieved

olive oil, for deep frying
sugar, to taste

Bring the water and salt to the boil. Remove the pan from the heat and pour in all the flour. Beat the mixture well, until it pulls away from the sides of the pan and forms a mass. Heat the olive oil in a pan until it is very hot, about 180°C (350°F) on a deep-fat thermometer, or until a small cube of stale bread dropped into the oil turns golden in 1 minute. Put the paste into a piping bag fitted with a star nozzle and pipe 8″ lengths into the oil, cutting them with a knife or scissors. Only do a few lengths at a time and fry for 5–8 minutes or until they are crisp and golden brown. Using a slotted spoon remove the churros to kitchen paper to drain. Sprinkle them with sugar and serve while they are still warm.

TORTAS DE ACEITE
(SESAME SEED AND ANISEED BISCUITS)

Most people probably only think of using olive oil in savoury dishes but it is so versatile it can equally well be used in sweet dishes as well. These spicy little biscuits are perfect with coffee.

To make 24 biscuits

1½ cups olive oil	½ cup sugar
thinly pared rind of ½ lemon	5 cups flour
1tbs sesame seeds	1tsp ground cinnamon
1tbs aniseeds	1tsp ground cloves
½ cup dry white wine	1tsp ground ginger
2tsp grated lemon rind	⅓ cup flaked almonds
2tsp grated orange rind	

Heat the olive oil in a saucepan until a light haze forms above it. Remove the pan from the heat and add the pared lemon rind, sesame seeds and aniseeds and leave to cool. Remove the lemon rind and pour the oil mixture into a large bowl. Add the wine, lemon and orange rind and sugar and beat until well blended and the sugar has dissolved. Sift the flour and spices into the bowl a little at a time, beating well until they form a soft dough. Using your hands, lightly knead the dough until it is smooth. Form into a ball and wrap in greaseproof paper. Set aside at room temperature for 30 minutes.

Preheat the oven to 200°C (400°F), Gas Mark 6. Line two large baking trays with non-stick cooking parchment. Remove the dough from its wrapping and divide into 24 equal pieces. Roll the pieces into small balls and using the palm of your hand, flatten them into flat round biscuits about ¼″–½″ thick. Arrange the biscuits on the prepared baking trays and press a few flaked almonds into the top of each one. Put the trays into the oven and bake for 15–20 minutes or until the biscuits are firm to the touch and golden brown round the edges.

ITALY

*I*taly is synonymous in most people's minds with olive oil. Looking back through history we see there are plenty of good reasons for this. As much a part of the people as the countryside, the olive probably first came to Italy from Sicily in the 6th or 7th century BC, and gradually it flourished in the ideal climate and varied soils of the peninsula. The Ancient Romans were the most influential in spreading the cultivation of the olive tree throughout the rest of Europe and North Africa, during the growth of their empire. They perfected curing techniques for olives and by the invention of the screw press,

Chianti symbol at Greve, Tuscany

developed the method for producing olive oil which has changed little in 2000 years.

But it wasn't only commerce which spurred the classical Roman interest in olives and olive oil. The Romans were famous for their feasts and indeed they are credited with producing one of the first cookery books, compiled by Apicius, a nobleman and great gourmet, living in the 1st century AD. He spent, so the story goes, his entire fortune on good food and wine! But he did leave behind a legacy of original culinary ideas and even established a cookery school.

It wasn't, however, until the Renaissance that this book was published officially; for along with the revival of art and literature during this period, went a renewed interest in food and cooking. The Renaissance flourished most magnificently in Tuscany and in the 19th century, when the first tourists made their pilgrimage to Florence, it was not only the beauty of the paintings and architecture which captured their imagination, but also the delights of the palate.

Tourists returning from Tuscany, since the days of the 'Grand Tour' have made the olive oils and wines famous beyond Italian shores. Unquestionably, it is olive oil which characterises Tuscan food because the dishes are simple — this is the centre for Italian cattle farming and the meat bred here is roasted, grilled or fried, without elaborate sauces.

The pine tree clad hills of Tuscany produce green olive oils of intense emerald beauty, whose odours are the very essence of the olive and whose flavours are rich and fruity. Epicures claim that the most celebrated oils come from Lucca, that ancient, aristocratic town resting serenely on the plain, but today there are excellent olive oils from every province in the region, pressed from the Frantoio, Leccino and Moraiolo varieties. Olive trees grow side by side with vines in Tuscany, because of course, this is the home of Chianti. So it's not surprising to find many of the best olive oils come from olives grown by some of the most eminent winemakers, who apply the same loving care and attention to both.

One such producer is Piero Stucchi Prinetti's family estate, Badia a Coltibuono. The name means Abbey of the Good Harvest and they have been producing Chianti for nearly 1000 years. The oil mill is on a beautiful old estate, surrounded by forests of fir, pine, oak and chestnut. It includes an 11th century abbey and several 15th century houses. Tuscan beauty at its most picturesque. The olives are picked by hand and any which are bruised or have fallen to the ground are rejected. After pressing, the oil is filtered through cotton, for, even though this filter absorbs more oil, they have found this to be the best method. The oil is then packed in hand-blown and numbered bottles.

Fattoria dell'Ugo is another Tuscan wine and olive oil producer. Situated, like Badia a Coltibuono, half way between Florence and Siena, the 17th century villa which is the family home forms part of an estate which has been in the Amici Grossi family for six generations.

An olive oil which has received a lot of recent praise, is Poggio Lamentano. This is produced from Moraiolo, Frantoio, Pendolino and Leccino olives grown on the rocky soil of the hills overlooking Castagnato Carducci, in Livorno province. Mr Zyw and his family came from Scotland in 1961, looking for a studio, where he could paint. As was common all over Italy at this time, many estates had been abandoned by Italian families who migrated to the larger towns, to earn a living. The Zyws settled in Castagnato Carducci and started producing oil from the trees on their estate. The olives are pressed

Fattoria dell'Ugo estate near Poggibonsi

at the local mill and the oil is bottled back at the family farm.

Poggio Lamentanto is one of the very few olive oils bearing the date of pressing, which means you can actually discover how different each year can be. I have tasted the 1985, which was smooth, mellow and fruity and the 1987, which was totally different; sharper and more bitter — once again ample proof that every bottle of olive oil is a new experience and only by constant testing will you discover your own preferences.

But travel through Italy and you will realise that every region produces olive oil, and each will claim that theirs is the best. The majority of single estate, extra virgin olive oils available in the stores at the moment come from Tuscany, merely because here, there has been a regional policy to establish strict standards of quality and promote the product. No doubt this will extend with time to other regions.

Meanwhile olive oils from Umbria, Apulia. Liguria and Molise are finding their way onto the shelves of imaginative, independent food shops. Look out for some of these and try them when you can.

Without doubt one of the most delicious, fruity olive oils I tasted is made by Stephano Caroli, in the town of Martina Franca in Apulia. Apulia in the south is the largest producer of olive oil, having more olive groves than any other region. It alone produces about 30% of the national output. The predominant variety grown here, along the narrow coastal plain and upland slopes, is the Coratina. Said to give the best extra virgin in Italy, it has a delicate fragrance and a taste that leaves you in no doubt that this is the juice of the olive, but at the same time it has a much softer flavour than the peppery Tuscan oils. I would certainly vote the olive oils from this part of Italy my personal favourites.

Umbria, one of the smallest regions of Italy, is rightly famed

Siena

for its extra virgin olive oils. Castello di Almonte is an Umbrian oil currently available in some shops and stores; and made from the Moraiolo, Leccino and Frantoio varieties, rich green in colour, tasty and peppery in flavour. The main areas of olive growing in this region are around Lake Trasimeno, Spoleto and Trevi, where the trees cloak the landscape with the vines which produce Orvieto wine.

Italy probably has the greatest diversity of olives anywhere in the world, to match the diversity of terrain. Some varieties of olives do thrive better in certain conditions than others, and this accounts for the abundance of different cultivars in Italy, which have developed as a result of the soil, altitude and exposure to the sun. It is difficult to give an accurate picture of all the varieties grown, however, because many regions give them their own names and some cultivars are particular to certain regions only.

Sadly, the winter of 1984/85, which in the northern hemisphere, was one of the coldest and harshest on record, severely damaged many trees in all olive-growing countries, but especially Italy, where it could take up to five years for the trees to recover.

Over recent years, many small, family producers have cut down their olive trees and replaced them with vines because of the growing market for wine and the high labour costs involved in harvesting olives — also because the market for olive oil has come to be dominated by large commercial producers, who can afford the enormous budgets necessary for promotion and new technology. The names of Berio, Sasso and Bertolli can be seen on shelves the world over. They provide national brands of consistent flavour and quality, but do not have the variety of flavours of the single estate olive oils which are really the equivalent of chateau-bottled wines.

One major factor to be aware of in the case of Italian oils, is that Italian law allows olive oils imported from other countries to be re-exported without stating the source. So in some cases you may be buying a bottle which has produce of Italy on the label, but the oil could well have come from Spain! This will not be the case if you buy cold pressed extra virgin from a single estate producer.

The Italians produce four types of virgin oils:

- OLIO EXTRAVERGINE D'OLIVA, maximum 1% acidity
- OLIO SOPRAFFINO VERGINE D'OLIVA, acidity 1%–1.5%
- OLIO FINO VERGINE D'OLIVA, acidity 1.5%–3%
- OLIO VERGINE D'OLIVA, acidity 3%–4%.

These are worth setting down here, because you might be misled into thinking that olio vergine d'oliva is the best, or indeed that olio d'oliva is a virgin olive oil, when in fact it is a refined and blended oil.

However, in Italy there are flavours to please every palate, as here there is probably the greatest diversity of olives to be found anywhere in the world. Indeed, many people say that Tuscan oils are the finest. I would not go so far. Olive oil is very much a matter of personal taste and to compare the olive oils of different countries is, I think, invidious. Added to which nearly every bottle of virgin oil is different depending on when the olives were harvested. It is certainly true, though, that the oils of Italy offer a different organoleptic experience from the golden oils of Spain, the robust oils of Greece and the fruity oils of Provence, but who is to say which is best since they are all the product of different olives, different soils and different climates.

Italian regional cuisine offers, perhaps more than in any other Mediterranean country, dishes where olive oil is shown off to best advantage. The Italians serve oil separately with many soups to be poured on as a condiment at the table. This recognises olive oil, not just as something to cook with, but as a flavouring in its own right. A dish as simple as pasta tossed in olive oil and garlic, needs no additions, other than being complemented by a robust red wine.

RIBOLLITA
(TUSCAN VEGETABLE SOUP)

 Ribollita literally means reboiled and it usually consists of leftovers from the day before reheated with the addition of beans. You can make it from scratch with any vegetables available and leave it overnight. In Tuscany, olive oil is served as a condiment to be poured onto the soup at the table, so this should be accompanied by a jug of your best olive oil.

To serve 6

½ cup dried cannellini beans
1 onion, chopped
1 carrot, chopped
1 stick celery, chopped
1 leek, chopped
3 tomatoes, peeled and chopped
3 cloves of garlic
2 cups diced courgettes

¼lb green beans, topped, tailed
 and cut into short pieces
6 slices of white bread
1lb green cabbage, sliced
olive oil
water
salt and pepper, to taste

Start preparing this dish the day before you want the soup. Put the dried beans in a pan with 900ml (1½pt) of cold water and bring to the boil. Then turn off the heat and leave them to soak for an hour. Heat some olive oil in a large pan and add the garlic, onion, carrot, celery and leek and saute gently for 5 minutes. Add the drained beans, the tomatoes and 1.8 litres (3pts) of cold water. Simmer gently for an hour or until the beans are tender. Half way through cooking the beans add the courgettes and green beans. Leave the soup overnight. The next day cook the cabbage in boiling water and reheat the soup. Put a slice of bread in the bottom of individual, warmed soup dishes. Drain the cabbage and pile onto the bread. Adjust seasoning of the soup to taste and ladle into the soup dishes. Serve with a jug of olive oil so that each person can pour some onto their soup.

PAPPA AL POMODORO
(TOMATO SOUP)

 This is a Tuscan soup, the main ingredients being stale bread and tomatoes. It is a soup of peasant origins and, like so many of these regional Italian dishes, it shows the ingenuity in combining a few basics and creating a simple but delightful meal. It is finished off with a dressing of olive oil.

To serve 4

3 large cloves of garlic, sliced
1½lb tomatoes, peeled, seeded and chopped
10oz bread, a few days old

3¾ cups water
large bunch of fresh basil leaves
olive oil
salt and pepper, to taste

Heat some olive oil in a pan, add the garlic and cook gently for about 5 minutes. Add the tomatoes and simmer for 15 minutes. Break the bread into small pieces and add to the pan along with the basil. Cover with water and simmer for 15 minutes. Season with salt and pepper.

The flavour of the soup improves if left overnight. So it can either be reheated or served cold. At the table pour over some olive oil.

Estate in Tuscany

BAGNA CAUDA
(HOT GARLIC AND ANCHOVY SAUCE)

 A classic sauce from Piedmont which is for true garlic lovers only. The name means 'hot bath' and it is served in the same way as a fondue, in a pot on the centre of the table over a candle, surrounded by raw vegetables, which are dipped into the sauce. It makes a wonderfully convivial meal for a group of friends and should be served with plenty of full-bodied red wine and good crusty bread.

To serve 6–8

$\frac{1}{4}$ cup butter
5 cloves of garlic, finely sliced

8 anchovy fillets in oil, drained
1 cup olive oil

Heat the butter in the serving pot or a small saucepan and add the garlic. Keep on a low heat so that the garlic does not brown. Add the anchovies and stir well, then gradually add the oil. Cook for about 10 minutes, over a low heat, stirring constantly. Place on the table over a candle or spirit lamp. Serve with a selection of washed and trimmed raw vegetables such as sliced peppers, celery, fennel, cauliflower, mushrooms, or carrots.

CAPONATA
(AUBERGINE SALAD)

 A Sicilian dish which can be served as an antipasti. It can also be stored in glass jars which should then be sealed and boiled for 20 minutes, after which it will keep for months.

1lb aubergines, cut into cubes
2tbs olive oil
4 sticks of celery, sliced
1 onion, sliced
8oz tomatoes, peeled and chopped
2tbs capers

2tbs pine nuts
1tbs sugar
$\frac{1}{2}$ cup red wine vinegar
$\frac{1}{4}$ cup large green olives
salt and pepper, to taste

Sprinkle the cubes of aubergine with salt and leave them in a colander to drain for an hour. Then dry them thoroughly on a kitchen towel. Heat plenty of olive oil in a pan and fry the aubergines until they are brown. Drain on kitchen paper. Fry the celery in the same oil as the aubergines and when brown remove from the pan. Add the onion and cook until soft, add the tomatoes and cook gently for 10 minutes. Add all the other ingredients, return the aubergine and celery to the pan and simmer for a further 5 minutes. Allow it to go cold before serving.

PEPERONI RIPIENI
(PEPPERS STUFFED WITH TOMATOES, TUNA, ANCHOVIES AND OLIVES)

This is a dish I have been serving for years. It encompasses all that I love about Italy and the stuffing for the peppers is so good I've usually eaten half of it before I start filling the peppers!

To serve 4

4 large red or green peppers
4tbs olive oil
1 onion, sliced
2 cloves of garlic, crushed
1½lb fresh tomatoes, peeled or
  tinned peeled tomatoes
2tbs tomato puree
a few leaves of fresh basil or
  ½tsp dried basil

½tsp oregano
1tbs parsley, chopped
12oz tin of tuna in olive oil,
  drained
4 anchovy fillets, chopped
12 black olives, stoned and halved
2tsp capers
⅓ cup Parmesan, grated
salt and pepper, to taste

Preheat the oven to 170°C (325°F), Gas Mark 3. Slice the tops from each pepper. Remove and discard the pith and seeds. Remove the stems from the sliced pepper tops and dice the flesh. Heat the olive oil in a pan and add the onion, garlic and diced pepper. Saute until the onion is soft. Stir in the tomatoes, tomato puree, herbs, salt and pepper and cook for 10 minutes. Stir in the rest of the ingredients except the cheese and cook for a further 10 minutes. Spoon the mixture into the peppers. Pour about ¼" of olive oil into a baking tray and arrange the peppers standing upright on the tray. Bake for about 30 minutes or until the peppers are soft, basting occasionally with the oil in the tray. When the peppers are cooked, sprinkle the Parmesan cheese on top of the filling and bake for a further five minutes. Remove from the oven and serve immediately.

PEPERONI ARROSTITI
(PEPPER SALAD)

 This simple salad can be served as part of an antipasti, but I especially like to serve it in the summer to accompany barbequed fish and meat. Its only dressing is olive oil so use a fruity one.

To serve 4–6

2 each red, yellow and green
  peppers

2 cloves of garlic, chopped
olive oil

Blacken the skins of the peppers by holding them over a gas flame or placing under a very hot grill. Remove the skins and wash the peppers. Cut into wide strips and remove the seeds and pith. Sprinkle with garlic and cover with olive oil.

PIZZA ALLA SICILIANA

 I suppose the era of fast food establishments has resulted in more people sampling a greater variety of cuisines, but sadly this has also meant certain dishes have become ubiquitous and pizza is definitely one of them. This is a pity because a really good pizza like this one is wonderful, filling, informal food especially when washed down with a bottle of red wine.

To serve 4–6

25g (1oz) fresh or 15g (½oz) dried
  yeast
⅔ cup warm water
pinch of sugar
4 cups strong flour
4tbs olive oil

1lb fresh, peeled or canned
  tomatoes, chopped
12 anchovy fillets
12 black olives, stoned and halved
salt, to taste

Mix the yeast with the warm water and a pinch of sugar, stir until it has dissolved and leave to stand until it foams. Sift the flour into a bowl with the salt and add the yeast mixture and a couple of tablespoons of olive oil. Work together with your hands until the mixture forms a rough ball, then knead to give a smooth, elastic dough. Put into an oiled bowl, cover with a damp cloth and leave in a warm place for about an hour, until doubled in bulk.

  Preheat the oven to 230°C (450°F) Gas Mark 8. When the dough has risen roll it out slightly, no more than ½″ thick, into one large circle or smaller individual ones. Place on well oiled baking trays. Cover the top of the dough with chopped tomatoes, and decorate with anchovies and olives. Drizzle over a few tablespoons of olive oil and bake for 15–20 minutes, or until the base is brown and crisp. Serve at once.

BRUSCHETTA or FETTUNTA

 One of the simplest but most superb of Italian snacks. This is the fare of the olive pickers and is a way of sampling the newly pressed oil.

1 large round crusty loaf of white bread, sliced thickly	cloves of garlic, peeled the best olive oil you can afford

Toast the slices of bread — if you can do it over an open fire all the better. Rub the toasted bread with a clove of garlic until it almost disappears and then drizzle over plenty of olive oil. Sprinkle with salt and pepper, to taste.

SPAGHETTI ALLA PUTTANESCA

 The sauce for this pasta comes from Naples and its name is not easily translatable into English because 'puttana' is a prostitute, so it means spaghetti in the manner of a prostitute. Make of that what you will, it's delicious nonetheless.

To serve 4

1lb spaghetti	1lb fresh tomatoes, peeled,
$\frac{1}{4}$ cup olive oil	seeded and chopped
2 cloves of garlic, sliced	1tbs capers
4 anchovy fillets, rinsed and	$\frac{2}{3}$ cup stoned black olives, sliced
chopped	1tbs parsley, chopped
1 small chilli pepper,	salt and pepper, to taste
seeded and chopped	

Cook the spaghetti in plenty of boiling salted water with a dash of olive oil. Heat the olive oil in a pan and add the garlic, anchovies and chilli, and cook for a few minutes. Add the tomatoes, capers and olives and simmer for 10 minutes until the sauce has thickened slightly. Stir in the parsley and cook for another minute. Drain the spaghetti and put into a warm bowl, pour over the sauce, toss the spaghetti in the sauce and serve immediately.

SPAGHETTI ALL'AGLIO E OLIO
(SPAGHETTI WITH GARLIC AND OIL)

Whilst every region in Italy has its own style of cooking, there is a basic difference between the North and South in their use of butter and olive oil. The South, being poorer, has always used olive oil more. This dish comes from Campania and the flavour of the olive oil is what makes it, so use your finest extra virgin.

To serve 4

1lb spaghetti
⅔ cup olive oil
3 large cloves of garlic, peeled
   and crushed

salt and pepper, to taste

Cook the spaghetti in plenty of boiling, salted water, with a dash of olive oil. Heat the olive oil with the cloves of garlic but do not let the garlic brown. Just warm the oil gently to release the flavour of the garlic. When the spaghetti is cooked, drain it and transfer to a warm serving bowl. Pour over the oil and garlic and toss the spaghetti well. Serve immediately.

SALMORIGLIO
(OLIVE OIL, LEMON AND GARLIC SAUCE)

This is a simple Sicilian dressing for grilled fish, usually swordfish. It can be served hot or cold and I use it sometimes as a salad dressing.

Makes about ⅔ cup

¼ cup water
⅔ cup olive oil
juice of 1 lemon

2 cloves of garlic, sliced
handful of parsley, chopped
1tsp oregano

Scald the water in a pan but do not boil. Put the olive oil into a bowl and beat in the water. Add the lemon juice, garlic, parsley and oregano and beat until the mixture is amalgamated. Place in a bain-marie and cook for 5 minutes, stirring the whole time.

CAPPON MAGRO
(FISH SALAD)

 The name suggests that this is a fasting dish; magro is a fast-day but nothing could be further from the truth. This is an elaborate Genoese salad incorporating fish and vegetables dressed in various ways with olive oil. It makes a spectacular centre piece for a dinner party or buffet because it's really only worth preparing for upwards of eight people. The variety of fish and vegetables used will depend on what is available.

To serve 8–10

1 loaf of white bread
garlic
8oz each of a selection of
    mushrooms, potatoes,
    cauliflower, carrots, artichoke
    hearts, green beans
1 head of celery
4lb fish made up of a selection of
    lobster, prawns, scallops,
    mussels, oysters, crab, salmon,
    and a white fish
olive oil
vinegar
lemon juice
salt

FOR THE SAUCE
1 large bunch of parsley, finely
    chopped
2 cloves of garlic
1tbs capers
4 anchovy fillets
2 yolks of hard boiled eggs
6 green olives, stoned
8floz olive oil
2tbs wine vinegar

FOR GARNISH
hard boiled eggs
olives

Cut the loaf of bread into sufficient slices to cover a large oval serving dish. Remove the crusts from the slices of bread and let them dry out in a low oven. Rub the slices with a clove of garlic and moisten with olive oil and a little vinegar.

Boil the vegetables until they are *al dente*. When they are cooked dress them with a vinaigrette made with olive oil, lemon juice and salt.

Poach the fish and shellfish and again do not overcook the fish, as it needs to be firm and not a soggy mass. Dress the fish in the vinaigrette.

To make the sauce, put all the ingredients except the olive oil in a blender and process to a smooth paste, then add the oil a little at at time until you have a sauce the consistency of thick cream.

Arrange the slices of bread on the serving dish and pour a little of the sauce over it. Then arrange the vegetables in the middle, surrounded with the fish and shellfish and pour over the remaining sauce. Serve immediately with the garnishes of your choice.

PASTA SALAD WITH BLACK OLIVES

 I first spotted this recipe by Arabella Boxer in *Vogue* years ago and have been serving it regularly ever since, either as a simple supper dish or as one of a number of dishes for an informal Mediterranean-style dinner. It not only looks beautiful, and tastes delicious but is very quick to make. All the ingredients are found in my store cupboard, so if someone drops in and stays to eat, this is often what I prepare.

To serve 4

1lb penne or rigatoni
1 cup olive oil
14oz tin of tomatoes
2 cloves of garlic, crushed
12oz tin tuna fish in oil, drained

2oz can anchovy fillets in oil,
   drained and chopped
12 black olives
salt and black pepper, to taste

Cook the pasta in plenty of salted boiling water with a dash of olive oil. When it is *al dente* drain and tip into a serving bowl. While it is still hot pour over the olive oil and toss well. Put the tomatoes with their juice and the garlic into a blender and process until you have a thick sauce, then stir into the pasta, adding salt and black pepper. Add the flaked tuna fish and anchovies. Then stir in the black olives. Serve warm, or cold, but do not refrigerate.

PESTO

 This is without question my favourite sauce for pasta, and I like it so much I often serve it at parties as a dip with raw vegetables.

The home of pesto is Genoa since basil flourishes all over Liguria and like so many of these classic recipes there are endless variations. The version I use has pine kernals but it can equally well be made without.

4 cups fresh basil leaves
1 clove of garlic
1tbs pine kernals
$\frac{1}{3}$ cup Parmesan, freshly grated

$\frac{1}{3}$ cup Pecorino, freshly grated
5tbs olive oil
salt, to taste

Put the basil, garlic and pine nuts, and cheese in a blender, add a dash of oil to make it run more easily and then with the motor running add the rest of the oil slowly until you have a thick cream. Add salt to taste.

If you are serving the pesto with pasta or in minestrone, thin it a little first with water from the pasta or some of the liquid from the soup.

AGNELLO CON OLIVE NERE
(LAMB WITH BLACK OLIVES)

This Tuscan dish has a superb, thick sauce laced with olives. Rabbit and chicken can be cooked in the same way, and in some recipes oregano is used instead of rosemary.

To serve 4

2lb lean, boneless lamb
3 cloves of garlic, crushed
1–2 sprigs fresh rosemary
2 tomatoes, peeled or 1tbs tomato
    puree

12 black olives, stoned
scant 1 cup dry white wine
4tbs olive oil

Cut the meat into cubes. Heat the olive oil in a casserole and add the garlic, cook for a few minutes until it is brown, then add the lamb and stir round until the meat is browned. Add the rosemary, tomatoes, olives and wine. Stir well, cover and cook for 30–40 minutes until the meat is tender and the sauce has thickened.

PRESERVES

Olive oil has been used since ancient times for preserving. It is ideally suited for this purpose; being liquid it forms a layer which seals the food off from the air. The added bonus is that if you preserve aromatic herbs or spices they flavour the oil deliciously. If you grow your own vegetables, you can keep them for months in jars of oil, but also you can buy produce from the markets when it is most plentiful. What could be better than your own tomato sauce made in the summer when tomatoes are cheap.

A few years ago when I had a particularly successful crop of basil, I happened to mention to the owner of my local Italian delicatessen that I had so much I didn't know what to do with it all and what a pity it would be to waste it. He told me that his mother preserved basil in jars of olive oil. Miracle of miracles. It is wonderful because the basil keeps its flavour, as well as flavouring the oil, which can be used for cooking or salad dressings.

All you do is pack a jar with basil leaves and pour in enough olive oil to fill the jar. It is best to put a layer of leaves in, pour in some oil and repeat the layers until the jar is full, making sure that the oil covers the leaves.

The same treatment can be applied to any of the herbs growing in the garden; try putting a sprig of rosemary, thyme or marjoram in a jar with olive oil. Create your own special combinations with garlic, crushed coriander seeds, chilli peppers, bay leaves, orange or lemon zest. You have the power of alchemy when you start to experiment with olive oil.

Make your favourite tomato sauce and pack it in a jar topped with olive oil.

Buy the tiny artichokes which appear in the shops in the summer. Boil them with water, vinegar and seasoning until they are tender. Drain and preserve covered with olive oil.

If you are an expert mushroom gatherer in the autumn, make a marinade of lemon juice, garlic, bay leaves, peppercorns, water and olive oil, boil it for 15 minutes, then add the mushrooms. Simmer for a further 5 minutes. Let the mushrooms cool in the marinade, drain and then bottle with olive oil.

FRITTO MISTO
(MIXED FRY)

 Olive oil is perfect for deep frying because it can reach high temperatures without deterioration. When food is fried in batter, as with this classic Italian dish, the oil enables the immediate formation of a protective coating thereby preventing the food absorbing excessive oil. Fritto Misto is another dish where the ingredients and proportions depend on personal taste. You can include chicken breasts, aubergines, mozzarella cheese and mushrooms.

To serve 4–6

8oz calf's brains	4 artichokes
8oz lamb's kidney	1 cup flour
8oz calf's liver	2tbs olive oil
8oz veal	$\frac{2}{3}$ cup water
1 small cauliflower, broken into florets	1 egg white
	salt, to taste
4 small courgettes, cut into $\frac{1}{4}$ inch slices	olive oil for frying
	lemon wedges

Start by making the batter an hour in advance because it needs time to stand. Put the flour, salt and oil in a blender and process, then gradually add the water. Leave to stand for an hour. Process again for a few seconds and fold in the beaten egg white, just before using the batter.

Soak the calf's brain in cold water for 30 minutes. Then place in a saucepan with enough water to cover, and add 1tbs of lemon juice or vinegar. Bring to the boil and simmer for 10 minutes. Remove from the heat, drain and immediately plunge into cold water. Drain and pat dry. Remove any of the outer membrane being careful not to tear the brains. Cut into cubes.

Cut the kidney, veal and liver into similar sized pieces. Remove the outer leaves from the artichokes, leaving the hearts. Remove the chokes and divide the hearts into quarters. Drop the artichoke pieces into cold water with a little lemon juice to prevent them from turning brown. When you are ready to fry them, remove from the water and pat dry.

Heat the olive oil to 180°C (350°F) in a deep fat fryer and preheat the oven to 110°C (225°F), Gas Mark $\frac{1}{4}$. Drop a few pieces of the meat into the batter. When they are well coated, remove with a slotted spoon and allow the excess batter to drain off. Deep fry for about 5 minutes until the batter is golden brown. Remove each batch to the oven to keep warm. Repeat this process until you have fried all the ingredients. Serve immediately garnished with the lemon wedges.

FOCCACIA
(FLAT BREAD)

 Every region in Italy has a different version of this delicious bread which is like a pizza dough. It can be flavoured with sage, crushed olives and onions or topped like a conventional pizza with tomatoes and cheese. This is the plain version just flavoured with olive oil and dimpled on the top. The aroma of the dough and the fruity oil when it is cooking makes it difficult to leave it long enough to cool! It is excellent with cheese or served with antipasti.

To serve 4–6

1oz fresh yeast
$\frac{2}{3}$ cup warm water
4 cups strong flour

6tbs olive oil
salt, to taste

Dissolve the yeast in the warm water. Put the flour into a large bowl and pour in the yeast, salt and 45ml (3tbs) of the olive oil. Knead these together until you have a smooth, soft, pliable dough. Cover, and leave to rise in a warm place until the dough has about doubled in size. Knock back the dough and knead for a few minutes. Roll out the dough to about $\frac{1}{2}''$ thick and lay it on a well oiled rectangular baking tray. Cover with a damp cloth and allow it ro rise again for about 30 minutes. Meanwhile preheat the oven to 200°C (400°F), Gas Mark 6. Before putting into the oven, dimple the top by pressing the dough with your finger tips and pour over the remaining olive oil. Bake for 20–30 minutes.

FRANCE

'*P*rovence is a painter's paradise and its tree, the olive is the painter's tree.' Aldous Huxley's simple but evocative description of the heart of France's olive-growing region, points to the great beauty of the countryside — the strong, sunny colours and the cornucopia of good things which spring from the soil. The hills are clad in wild fragrant rosemary, thyme and fennel. Fields of blue

sweet-smelling lavender sway gently in a light summer breeze, against serried ranks of giant yellow sunflowers.

Here, you find tiny villages in ochre and faded pinks, clinging to the mountain sides, dotted with window boxes of bright red cascading geraniums. In the centre of a village square, you might find a fountain trickling languidly and perhaps nearby under the shade of gnarled olive trees, a leisurely game of boules progressing slowly, the navy berets of the players nodding sagely. Nimble goats graze on rocky outcrops, bells tinkling in the clear air. The soporific hum of flies and honey bees in the midday sun. And all around are colours, sounds, smells and above all, tastes from the rich wines, perfumed melons, creamy white goat's cheeses and black oily olives. An area of so many contrasts — from the teeming hustle of the coast to the inland region with its mountains, hills, gorges, plains and ever present pine trees.

Throughout the region you will find stone olive oil mills; some have been abandoned; others, like La Balmeenne in Beaumes-de-Venise have been modernised, or like Ludovic Alziari's in Nice are working much as they were hundreds of years ago producing light fruity oils which can be bought from them directly.

But undoubtedly the olive town of Provence is Nyons, surrounded by a protective ring of mountains and sitting astride the River Eygues. The town, with its 14th century bridge, enjoys a special microclimate where plants and people alike thrive, protected from the excesses of the mistral. There are old mills operating much as they did in Roman times, and the local oil co-operative produces and sells award-winning extra virgin as well as fleshy black olives, the only ones in France to carry an appelation d'origen. There is a lively market every Thursday where you will find on sale most of the olives grown in the region. Here is some information about the different varieties available if you should be lucky enough to shop there.

🜚 PICHOLINE. The main green French variety. The fruit is small and long. The colour ranges between green and yellow-green. A tasty, firm-fleshed olive which grows in the Gard and Bouches-du-Rhone regions.

LUCQUES. A very good table olive probably originating from Lucques in Italy. The fruit is long and curved, the flesh is green and glossy. It grows mainly in the Herault.

TANCHE. This is *the* olive of Nyons. It was introduced after the freeze of 1956 to Provence, the Ardeche and Corsica. Produces lots of oil and is resistant to the cold. The large, delicious olives are picked when black for the table.

CAILLETIER. Also known as the olive of Nice. This is a famous tiny, smooth black olive with a wonderful aroma.

Olives are such a part of life here that in January or February, depending on the time of the harvest, there is a Fete de L'Alicoque, a celebration to welcome the new crop. You really must visit!

Travelling on towards the coast, through valleys whose slopes are clad with olive and almond trees, you come to Maussane nestling at the feet of Les Alpilles. This has another famous co-operative, thought by many to produce the finest oil in the whole of France, a fragrant olive oil marketed under the name of La Vallee des Beaux. Not far from here is the small town of Fontvielle, made famous by Alphonse Daudet, in his *Lettres de mon Moulin*. The mill is preserved today as a museum.

Many of France's most accomplished writers and painters have made the olive the subject of their art. Marcel Pagnol's novels recently made into two enormously successful films, 'Jean de Florette' and 'Manon des Sources', depict the harsh struggle of the Provencal farmer against the elements. Jean Giono reflected 'The olive grove represents a library where one goes to forget life or to understand it better', and he wrote a great deal about the mystery and beauty of the eternal tree. He was posthumously made honorary president of the 'Confrerie des Chevaliers de Olivier', an association of all the olive growers in the region. Who but the French would honour a writer in such a way?

It is indicative of the laudable French approach to food and wine, that they do not consider it too lowly a subject for literature or painting. Renoir once remarked, 'Regardez cette lumiere dans les oliviers: ca brille comme un diamant'. Van Gogh painted many, many pictures of olive trees. But he did not find them easy

Nyons market

subjects. 'I struggle to capture this', he wrote. 'It is silver, a while ago more blue, on the whole green, whitish bronze, against the yellow, rose, purplish-blue, orange, ochre-red earth.'

It was the Phoenician Greeks who when they founded Massalia — modern day Marseilles — in about 6000 BC, brought the olive tree with them. It spread throughout the South of France with the arrival of the Romans, who called the region Provence — their first province beyond the Alps.

Today, Provence consists of five departments — Bouches du Rhone, Vaucluse, Alpes de Haute Provence, Alpes Maritimes and Var, all of them the major olive-growing areas. Here, too, sprung up a great French industry from the olive oil trade — the final pressing, inferior oil goes to make soap. Today, the savon de Marseille, invented by the French in the first century, is famous all over the world.

Surprisingly perhaps, France is actually one of the world's smallest producers. In order to meet home demand, she imports 26,000 tonnes of olive oil a year from Spain, Italy, Tunisia and Morocco. Interestingly, the French only consume 0.4 litres of olive oil per head each year, as against the Italians' 11 litres and the Greeks' 21 litres. The reputation of its home produced oil, however, is extremely high. Scarcity value perhaps!

But the olive industry in France has suffered over the last 60 years from natural enemies, and a change in the market forces.

The big 'freezes' of 1929 and 1956 affected the trees badly. Moreover, the olive trees in the South of France have been cut down to make way for the now more profitable vine.

The olive industry in France consists entirely of some 45,000 small producers, who take their olives to local mills or co-operatives. There are no Bertollis or Carbonells to buy up the crops, and market them on an international scale. This is one reason why you do not find that many French olive oils outside France. The small farmer just doesn't have the resources to advertise and ship his product overseas. The competition from seed oils, at much lower prices, has also been an added difficulty for the small producer and has encouraged the French housewife to abandon olive oil in favour of sunflower and peanut oil.

Even if the French housewife does not hold olive oil in high regard, gourmets do and claim that there are two elements in Provencal cooking, olives and garlic — which supports the Provencal saying 'a fish lives in water and dies in olive oil'!

When you travel through Provence you will taste so many traditional dishes, in which olive oil plays a major role. Dishes like Bouillabaisse, a rich fish stew which purists claim cannot be made out of the South of France. This is because Rascasse, a tiny rock fish and the essential ingredient, giving the dish its unique flavour, is only found along these coastal waters. Peppers, courgettes and aubergines grown locally in abundance appear in Ratatouille, the vegetable stew. Touiller in Provencal means to stir and Tatouille, to stir a second time, which is exactly what you have to do when preparing this dish. The French in this part of the country even manage to create their own form of butter from olive oil, by putting a cup of oil in the fridge and letting it solidify. Soups are prevalent and one famous one, L'Aigo Boulido, is garlic boiled in water and poured over bread soaked in olive oil. It may not sound very appetising but it is supposed to be a marvellous cure for a hangover!

Olive oil and soap shop. Marseilles

SOUPE AU PISTOU
(VEGETABLE SOUP WITH PISTOU)

I love making soups. I started making them in my student days because vegetable soups are filling, cheap and nourishing — a pound of carrots, some leeks and maybe some fresh herbs, if they are available, and you have a meal in half an hour! For this reason, it's a constant source of amazement why anyone buys ready-made soups even on the basis of convenience. My repertoire of soups for both summer and winter has grown over the years and this is one of my personal favourites. A friend of mine has always categorized my soups as queens, kings and aces. This is an ace!

To serve 4 or in my case 2 with second helpings

$\frac{2}{3}$ cup dried white haricot beans
water for soaking and boiling
    beans
1 onion, chopped
1 clove of garlic, crushed
$1\frac{1}{4}$ cups chopped tomatoes
$\frac{2}{3}$ cup diced carrot
$\frac{2}{3}$ cup diced potato
2 leeks, sliced
$\frac{1}{2}$ cup sliced celery
4oz French green beans
1 cup sliced courgettes

$\frac{1}{2}$ cup either broken spaghetti or
    small pasta for soups
$6\frac{1}{4}$ cups water
2tbs olive oil
salt and pepper, to taste

PISTOU
3 cloves of garlic
large bunch of basil leaves
$\frac{2}{3}$ cup freshly grated Parmesan
2tbs olive oil

Put the beans in a pan with plenty of cold water. Bring to the boil and then remove from the heat. Leave the beans to soak for 1 hour. Then cook until tender. Heat some olive oil in a large pan and cook the onion and garlic until golden brown. Add the tomatoes and cook for a few minutes. Pour in the water and bring to the boil. Add the carrots, potatoes, leeks and celery. Reduce the heat and simmer for 10–15 minutes. Meanwhile make the pistou. You can use a mortar and pestle or a blender. Mash the garlic and basil together. Add the cheese and then gradually beat in the olive oil. Put in the beans and their liquid, the green beans, courgettes and pasta into the soup. Simmer until tender. Season to taste. Put the pistou into a soup tureen and pour the soup over it. Leave the soup to stand for about 10 minutes to allow the pistou to favour it. Pistou should never be added to the soup while it is cooking and should be regarded as a condiment to be added as the final flourish.

AIGO BOULIDO
(BOILED WATER)

This Provencal soup is supposed to be a panacea for all ills and a marvellous cure for hangovers. There is an old saying 'Aigo Boulido sauova la vida'. Boiled water saves your life!

To serve 4

4 cups water
12 cloves of garlic
2 bay leaves
1 sprig of sage

4 tbs olive oil
salt, to taste
slices of dry white bread

Put all the ingredients, except the bread and 1 tbs of olive oil, into a saucepan and boil for 15 minutes. Remove the pan from the heat and let it stand for 5 minutes. Put slices of dry bread in the bottom of each soup plate, dribble over the remaining oil and pour over the soup.

SALAD NICOISE

A genuine Salad Nicoise is created solely from raw vegetables, but in many places today if you order this salad it will come with boiled potatoes and green beans. This is a pity because the salad should be crisp and fresh and I think it becomes rather heavy and soggy with cooked vegetables — but adding a can of flaked tuna fish is acceptable.

To serve 6 as a starter or 4 as a main dish

10 medium-sized tomatoes, cut
   into quarters
1 clove of garlic, peeled
1 cucumber, peeled and finely
   sliced
2 green peppers, pith and seeds
   removed, thinly sliced
6 spring onions, thinly sliced
12 anchovy fillets

$\frac{1}{4}$ cup black olives
3 hard boiled eggs, quartered
6 tbs olive oil
salt and pepper, to taste
a few shredded basil leaves

Sprinkle the tomatoes with salt and set on one side to drain. Cut the clove of garlic in half and rub a salad bowl well with the two halves. Make the dressing with the olive oil, salt, pepper and basil. Add all the ingredients including the drained tomatoes to a bowl and pour over the dressing.

RATATOUILLE

Even though all the vegetables that go into a ratatouille are available now, all the year round, I still think of this dish as heralding in the summer. It certainly contains the essence of the Mediterranean. I include it because it is inconceivable that it would taste as good as it does, without olive oil. It can be served hot or cold, as a main or side dish.

To serve 4 as a main or 6 as a starter

2lb aubergines, cut into cubes
1½lb courgettes, sliced
2 large green peppers, pith and
    seeds removed, cut into squares
1 large onion, sliced

2 large cloves of garlic, crushed
2lb tomatoes, peeled and seeds
    removed
olive oil
salt and pepper, to taste

Sprinkle the aubergines with salt and leave to drain for 10 minutes, then pat dry. Heat a good measure of olive oil in a pan and fry the aubergines quickly, so as to prevent them from soaking up too much oil, until they are light brown. Remove them from the pan. Repeat with the courgettes, peppers, onion and garlic, one after the other, adding more olive oil to the pan as necessary. When all the vegetables have been browned, return them to the pan and gently stir in the tomatoes, so they coat all the vegetables. Bring to the boil and then simmer gently until the vegetables are tender. Season to taste. Do not overcook them or you'll end up with a soggy stew. Each vegetable should hold its shape.

POMMES A L'HUILE

This is a wonderful, hot potato salad, to serve with fish, or the way I usually serve it, with boiled sausage. A dish in which you can use your fruitiest olive oil.

To serve 4

1lb new potatoes
handful of parsley, chopped
2 spring onions, sliced

3tbs olive oil
salt, to taste

Boil the potatoes in their skins, in salted water. When they are cooked, drain and put into a serving bowl. Stir in the parsley, onions and olive oil.

PAN BAGNAT

The olive growing regions of France follow a line round the south coast so it's not surprising to find that many recipes using olives and olive oil come from in and around Nice. This snack is really a salad nicoise in bread; pan bagnat means literally wet bread and this is ideal to take on a summer picnic.

1 long French loaf or individual
    rolls
1 clove of garlic
olive oil
wine vinegar, to taste
1lb tomatoes, sliced
1 onion, sliced

1 green pepper, deseeded and
    sliced
1 red pepper, deseeded and sliced
1 hard boiled egg, sliced
2–3 anchovy fillets
6 black olives, stoned
salt and pepper, to taste

Slice the loaf or rolls horizontally and scoop out a little of the bread to allow the filling to fit. Rub the inside of each half with the garlic, pour on a few drops of the vinegar and plenty of olive oil, salt and pepper. Fill the loaf with the tomatoes, onion, peppers, egg and anchovies. Press the top of the loaf on like a lid. Wrap in tin foil and put under a heavy weight for about 1 hour to allow the juices to seep into the bread.
Slice and serve.

PISSALADIERE

 This dish is a native of Nice and is similar to an Italian pizza. It is a bread dough base covered with a generous layer of onions, olives and anchovies. It can be made equally well on a shortcrust pastry base and this is the version I give here.

8oz shortcrust pastry
2½lb onions, finely sliced
2 cloves of garlic, crushed

10 anchovy fillets
12 black olives
2tbs olive oil

Preheat the oven to 200°C (400°F), Gas Mark 6. Roll out the pastry and line a 12″ oiled baking tray. Heat the olive oil in a pan, add the onions and garlic and cook very slowly until the onions are soft but not brown. Top the pastry with the cooked onions, decorate with the olives and anchovies. Dribble a little olive oil over the top and bake in the oven for about 20 minutes or until the pastry is cooked. Serve hot or warm.

MAYONNAISE

 It may seem rather obvious to have a recipe for mayonnaise, but I think it is worth including because it has to be the quintessential olive oil sauce. I personally find that the finest extra virgin oils are too flavourful to use in mayonnaise — they make the taste too rich — and so I usually opt for a good brand of pure olive oil. Pure olive oil is refined olive oil with some extra virgin added for taste, aroma and colour. So it's flavour is not too powerful.

2 egg yolks
1½tbs white wine vinegar or
   lemon juice

½tsp mustard
1¼ cups olive oil
salt and pepper, to taste

Blend together the egg yolks, mustard and vinegar or lemon juice in a food processor, then with the motor running add the olive oil very slowly in a thin stream. If the mayonnaise becomes too thick, thin it with either more vinegar and lemon juice or some warm water. The whole process is more assured of success if everything is at room temperature.

With a plain, homemade mayonnaise you can add all sorts of other ingredients, such as tomato puree, horseradish, anchovies, fresh herbs — basil, tarragon, dill, chervil or watercress for a beautiful green mayonnaise, which can be served with grilled fish, chicken or raw vegetables.

TAPENADE
(BLACK OLIVE PASTE)

This Provencal spread is delicious on toasted bread, and served as a canape or it is often used to stuff hard boiled eggs. Some recipes contain tuna fish but I think that just the flavour of the olives and anchovies is best.

1½ cups stoned black olives
2 cloves of garlic
8tbs capers, drained

4oz anchovy fillets
1tsp mustard
1tbs olive oil

If you think the anchovies are going to be too salty, soak them in milk for 10 minutes. Then place all the ingredients in a blender and mix to a smooth paste.

ANCHOIADE
(ANCHOVY PASTE)

Simply a mixture of garlic and anchovies which can be served on toasted slices of French bread, with drinks. If you can toast the bread over an open fire all the better!

4oz anchovy fillets
2 cloves of garlic

1–2tbs wine vinegar
2–3tbs olive oil

Place all the ingredients in a blender and mix to a smooth paste. If you think that the anchovies may be too salty, soak them first in milk for 10 minutes.

VINAIGRETTE

I make no apology for including a recipe for vinaigrette. Firstly, because like mayonnaise it is all about good olive oil, and secondly, because I think some people are under the delusion, especially in restaurants where they should know better, that it is about vinegar. I am often amazed at what is served up under the name of vinaigrette; a bowl of vinegar with a splash of olive oil. I now keep in my kitchen bottles of extra virgin olive oil from France, Spain, Greece and Italy and I treat them as if they were bottles of perfume. Each time I make a French dressing I decide what flavour and aroma I want depending on my mood. Extra virgin olive oil is about experimentation. If you don't only wear one fragrance then don't only stick to one olive oil.

⅔ cup olive oil   salt and pepper, to taste
1tbs wine vinegar or lemon juice

Beat the vinegar with salt and pepper until the salt dissolves and then beat in the olive oil a little at a time.

That's it. Simple and delicious.

You can of course add some mustard, crushed garlic or fresh herbs. I sometimes add brown sugar and soy sauce for a spicy vinaigrette or sour cream beaten in, to pour over cooked beetroot. I like to think of vinaigrette as a blank canvas to which you can add other colours from your kitchen palette.

AIOLI

This Provencal mayonnaise is made with as many cloves of garlic as you have a taste for. It is probably as well to ensure that you don't have any pressing social engagements the next day!

4–10 cloves of garlic, peeled and   1½–2tbs white wine vinegar or
     crushed   lemon juice
2 egg yolks   salt, to taste
1¼ cups olive oil

Put the garlic, egg yolks and a pinch of salt into a blender and process until smooth. Add the lemon juice or vinegar, process again and then gradually pour in the olive oil. If it is too thick, thin with a little more vinegar or lemon juice or warm water.

CHEVRES A L'HUILLE
(MARINATED GOAT'S CHEESE)

 You see large jars of tiny cheeses in olive oil on the counters of many delicatessens these days. It is more fun to prepare them yourself and to create your own personal combination of herbs.

small round goat's cheeses
   weighing about 2oz each
olive oil
a selection and combination of
   rosemary, cloves of

garlic, bay leaves, thyme,
   shallots, small black olives,
   chilli peppers, peppercorns

Put the goat's cheeses into a jar, loosely packed, tuck in your choice of aromatics and cover with oil. Leave for at least a couple of weeks.

FONDUE BOURGUIGNONNE

 The traditional Swiss fondue is made with cheese but in this French version, meat is speared on forks and cooked in boiling olive oil. It is served with a variety of dips and sauces. This is a friendly way to serve six people for supper and means that the hostess doesn't have too much rushing about!

To serve 6

3lb beef fillet, cubed
selection of spicy sausages cut into
   pieces

$1\frac{1}{4}$ cups olive oil

Heat the oil in a saucepan to 180°C (350°F) on a deep-fat thermometer, or until a small piece of stale bread dropped in turns golden brown in 40 seconds. Pour the oil into a fondue pot and place it on the table over a candle or spirit burner.

   Serve with salt and pepper, lemon wedges and three or four sauces such as green mayonnaise, mayonnaise with a little curry powder mixed in, a homemade tomato sauce or the traditional garlic mayonnaise - Aioli.

DAUBE DE BOEUF A LA PROVENCAL
(BEEF WITH OLIVES)

 Daubes are the wonderful beef stews found all over southern France. The sauce is thick and rich through long, slow cooking and by marinading the beef, the meat is tenderized. The best flavour is achieved by cooking the dish one day and reheating it the next.

To serve 6

3lb stewing steak, cubed
8oz streaky bacon, cut into strips
2 cups sliced mushrooms
1lb tomatoes, peeled, seeded and
  chopped
3 cloves of garlic, crushed
1tbs chopped parsley
1 piece of orange rind, 1–2"
1 bouquet garni
¾ cup beef stock
16 black olives, stoned and halved
flour

MARINADE
1¼ cups red wine
¼ cup brandy
1tsp black peppercorns
sprig of thyme
2 bay leaves
2 cloves of garlic, crushed
1 large onion, sliced
2 carrots, sliced
salt, to taste

Combine all the ingredients for the marinade in a large bowl and add the beef. Cover and place in the fridge overnight.

Blanch the bacon in boiling water for 5 minutes, drain and pat dry. Remove the beef from the marinade and pat dry, reserving the marinade. Preheat the oven to 160°C (325°F), Gas Mark 3. Toss the beef in the flour and shake off the excess. Arrange two or three strips of bacon over the bottom of a large casserole. Spoon over a few of the marinaded vegetables, followed by some of the mushrooms and tomatoes. Then add a layer of beef, sprinkle with garlic and parsley. Add the bouquet garni and the piece of orange rind. Continue making layers, finishing with a layer of bacon. Pour over the beef stock plus the marinade, and scatter with the olives. Bring to the boil and then place in the oven. Braise for about 4 hours until the meat is tender. Remove from the oven and skim off any fat. Serve at once or leave overnight and reheat.

GREECE

*I*magine the Mediterranean without the olive tree. What a different prospect it would offer. But surely of all the countries, Greece is the most difficult to picture! Every island and every region is mountainous. What would be barren and inhospitable, is softened and shaded by the moving grey-green mist of 120 million olive trees. They take the edges off the angles, and provide the backdrop to each tiny harbour and each whitewashed village. Imagine

sipping your glass of ouzo in the village square, without the relaxing shade of an olive tree.

The beauty of Greece is in its islands, its crystal clear sea, its blue cloudless skies and above all the sound of a breeze rustling the leaves of countless olive trees.

The olive is of unique importance in Greece. Legend tells that in the mighty contest, for the control of Attica, between Athena, goddess of wisdom and Poseidon, ruler of the seas, Athena's gift to mankind was the olive tree, Poseidon's, the horse. The gods chose the bountiful tree and Athena was honoured for all time by giving her name to the capital of Greece.

Since those ancient times the olive has flourished in a country where little else can grow. All over the rocky terrain of Greece, the olive tree has survived, boring its roots deep into the earth, providing not only its fruit but a livelihood for millions.

At every turn of the page in Greek history, the olive has been the foundation of the country's economy. The ancient Greeks traded oil for corn and precious minerals. They learned its use for light and medicine, and then for its culinary applications. Their craftsmen produced the most beautiful jars to hold this valuable commodity and lamps to burn it in. Its navy carried it throughout the Mediterranean. During the long Venetian occupation of the islands (1386–1797), the peasants were encouraged to plant olive trees and pay their taxes in olive oil. In many islands, a man's wealth was counted by the number of olive trees he owned, and land values in some places are even now based on the number of olive trees growing. Even today it occupies an equally central role in the well being of the country.

Odysseus once remarked that Greece is 'a rough land but a good nurse of men and I want no sweeter home'. Rough it is. The country, which stretches from Crete in the south to Thrace in the north, is mostly mountainous. It is characterised by a variety of climates, terrains and altitudes. The olive tree has adapted to these poor, rocky soils, where no cattle can graze and no other crops could survive the lack of rainfall and the heat of the sun. The olive symbolises hope and fertility, and seems to embody the spirit of a people who have survived wars, invasions and earthquakes, yet who remain proud, generous and friendly.

The importance of the olive varies from region to region. In Crete, olive trees occupy over 60% of the cultivated land, in the southern mainland, 30%, but in the north only 4%. Production is concentrated in the Peloponnese and Crete. One of the main towns in the Peloponnese is Kalamata, which is of course also the name of the main olive variety grown in Greece.

Many families rely heavily on olives and olive oil for their income. There are nearly 1 million farms in Greece and the greater part of these are engaged in olive growing. But the olive industry doesn't only employ a vast labour force for its cultivation; there are people working in the 3000 traditional and 400 modern mills, as well as the bottling and packing plants. There is no other crop in Greece which occupies so much available work force.

Olive cultivation is highly seasonal work; November to February is the harvest time and fits in ideally for the Greeks with the tourist season in the summer months. This means that families, who would have difficulty surviving on olive growing alone, can work on casual summer jobs or perhaps rent out rooms to the thousands of sun-seeking holidaymakers.

The market in Athens displays an amazing array of green olives, cracked and preserved in rigani, lemon and coriander; and black olives, especially the large juicy Kalamatas. Eighty per cent of the olives grown go to produce oil, and the rest are preserved as table olives. Europe and the USA have been enthusiastically devouring Greek olives for years but the olive oils have, as yet, not found the same favour. They are an acquired taste, being much more powerful and rustic than the oils of Spain or France but a perfect foil to Retsina. Maybe this is why the Greeks resinate their wine.

Olives are not used generally in Greek dishes, but they are eaten in abundance as a part of mezes and it is unusual to be served a drink without a dish of large, shining olives to accompany it.

I can't think of anything more enjoyable than sitting in a taverna on a warm summer's evening with a chilled bottle of Retsina, some grilled fish which has been cooked over an open fire, and a plate of green beans bathed in a pool of fruity olive oil, waiting to be mopped up with lashings of fresh bread.

FAKI SOUPA
(LENTIL SOUP)

 A few years ago when I was staying on the tiny island of Astipalaia, I was delighted to find this soup on the menu of one of the little tavernas. I love lentil soup but I had not come across it in Greece before. The owner, impressed by my enthusiasm for her cooking, gave me her recipe.

To serve 4

¾ cup brown lentils
1 large onion, sliced
2 cloves of garlic, crushed
3oz can of tomato puree
8oz fresh tomatoes, peeled and
   seeded

a good pinch of oregano
2tbs olive oil
3¾ cups water
salt and pepper, to taste

Cover the lentils with cold water and bring to the boil. Drain the lentils and return to the pan with 900ml (1½pts) of water, the garlic, onion, tomato puree, fresh tomatoes, oregano and olive oil. Bring to the boil and simmer until the lentils are soft. Remove from the heat and blend but not for long; the mixture should not be too smooth. Season to taste.

TARAMASALATA

 Tarama is dried, salted, grey mullet roe but as it is not easily available in this country, most people use smoked cod's roe. Like all these traditional dishes there are fierce debates about authentic recipes — some will say that it should not contain garlic, some recipes contain onion and so on. This is my preferred way.

4oz smoked cod's roe
2 slices of white bread, with crusts
   removed
cold water

½ small onion, sliced
juice of a large lemon
½ cup olive oil
black olives, to garnish

Soak the bread in cold water for 5 minutes, then squeeze dry. Skin the cod's roe and put in a blender, with the bread, onion and half the lemon juice and process. Gradually add the oil until you have a creamy paste. Add the rest of the lemon juice according to your taste. Garnish with some black olives and serve with warm pitta bread.

MELIZANOSALATA
(AUBERGINE SALAD)

This puree of aubergines is known in some places as 'poor man's caviar' and can be served as part of a mezes, the little portions of hot and cold food served with drinks. If you like aubergines this is a delicious way to serve them and they taste even better if baked on charcoal, so have a go at putting them on the fire the next time you have a barbeque.

To serve 4

1lb aubergines
1 small onion, sliced
1 clove of garlic, crushed
juice of 1 lemon

$\frac{1}{4}$ cup olive oil
parsley, chopped
black olives, to garnish

Preheat the oven to 200°C (400°F), Gas Mark 6. Prick the aubergines, put them on a baking tray and place in the oven until they are soft — about 1 hour depending on their size. Don't worry if the skins turn black as this gives a lovely smokey flavour to the dish. When they are cool enough to handle, scoop out the flesh and put into a blender with the garlic, onion and half the lemon juice. Blend well and add the oil until you have a thick paste. Add the rest of the lemon juice according to taste. Serve in a dish, garnished with the chopped parsley and olives.

SKORTHALIA
(GARLIC SAUCE)

This pungent garlic sauce is served in Greece with fried fish or vegetables. I have had it as an accompaniment with fried salt cod as a starter and found it compulsive eating.

3 slices of white bread,
crusts removed
cold water
3 large cloves of garlic

juice of $\frac{1}{2}$ lemon or
2tbs white wine vinegar
$\frac{1}{2}$ cup olive oil

Soak the bread in cold water for 5 minutes and squeeze dry. Put into a blender with the garlic, lemon juice or wine vinegar and process well. Gradually pour in the olive oil until you have a sauce the consistency of mayonnaise.

🫒

VEGETABLES A LA GRECQUE

 Some people describe the vegetable dishes from Greece as swimming in olive oil and that is exactly how they are meant to be — it is what makes them so good eaten cold. They can be cooked with a variety of aromatics but the essential ingredient is good Greek olive oil. This is a marinade I use to cook a selection of vegetables, which I serve as a starter with plenty of crusty bread to mop up the juices.

To serve 4–6

MARINADE
2½ cups water
2½ cups dry white wine
⅔ cup olive oil
juice of one lemon
2 cloves of garlic, crushed
2 bay leaves
½tsp coriander seeds
1 sprig of thyme
5 peppercorns
small handful of parsley sprigs

VEGETABLES
a selection from the following:
small artichokes, quartered;
button mushrooms; cauliflower;
bulb fennel; small pickling
onions

Bring the wine and water to the boil in a large pan and add all the other marinade ingredients. Reduce the heat and simmer for 15 minutes. Then throw in the vegetables, putting the longer cooking vegetables in first. Cook for about 10 minutes and then add the mushrooms and cauliflower and cook for about a further 5 minutes. Strain the liquid off from the vegetables, and boil to reduce to about half. Pour over the vegetables and refrigerate. Serve cold.

HORIATIKI
(GREEK COUNTRY SALAD)

Until a few years ago, I went to Greece seven years in succession. Though there are many Greek dishes I savour, this is the one I most associate with my many happy holidays.

To serve 4

1lb tomatoes, cut into quarters
½ cucumber, peeled and sliced
1 small green pepper, pith and
    seeds removed, thinly sliced
1 onion, thinly sliced

5oz feta cheese
12 black olives
a pinch of oregano
4tbs olive oil
salt and pepper, to taste

Place the tomatoes, cucumber, pepper and onion in a bowl. Dress with the olive oil, salt and pepper. Arrange the feta cheese and olives on the top and sprinkle on the oregano.

KOTOPOULO ME ELIES
(CHICKEN CASSEROLE WITH OLIVES)

This spicy casserole is based on one from Rena Salaman's excellent book *Greek Food*. She recommends using a boiling fowl as its long cooking time gives the spices time to flavour the meat.

To serve 4

1 boiling fowl or a jointed chicken
3tbs olive oil
⅔ cup of red wine
1 stick of cinnamon
3 cloves

salt and pepper, to taste
2 allspice
1 bay leaf
14oz can of tomatoes
16 black or green olives
salt and pepper, to taste

Wash and dry the chicken, season with salt and pepper and fry in the olive oil. Pour the wine into the pan, add the spices, bay leaf and tomatoes. Cover and simmer for 1 hour for chicken and about 2 hours for a fowl or until the meat is tender. Add the olives in the last 10 minutes, by which time the sauce should be thick. Serve with rice or pasta.

NORTH AFRICA

Despite the particular difficulties of growing olives in North Africa, Morocco, Tunisia and Algeria excel in their table olives.

Olives are picked at every stage of ripeness and the markets are resplendent with enormous bowls of green olives with pimiento and preserved lemons, pink olives, red olives, brown olives, and black olives, colours you never imagined olives could be. They are preserved

Moroccan market

in numerous different ways and you *have* to travel to these places to taste such delights, because they are prepared by local market holders to their own traditional recipes.

The Moroccans have long been masters in the use of spices and they treat their olives royally, preserving them with lemons, fennel, hot peppers, cumin, coriander and garlic. There really is a very limited selection of table olives available from our shops, stores and delicatessans, compared to the banquets of olives for sale in a market in Marrakesh or Meknes in Morocco. The tastes are exquisite, the flavours infinite. How inadequate words become when trying to describe the sense of taste.

Try to visit these countries if you are interested at all in olives because they will open up experiences of sight, sound and smell in their markets, which picking up a tin of olives in brine from your local supermarket can never match. Until you stand in a dusty, narrow medina, sampling olives in five different colours, bathed in five different marinades, you cannot appreciate what an extraordinary fruit the olive can be.

Morocco, Algeria and Tunisia all grow olives on a large scale, and in fact each of these countries grow far more olives than France, but because they don't find their way into Europe and the USA, they are not well known. The olive oils produced are mainly for domestic consumption, but both Morocco and Tunisia export to other Arab countries and Italy.

Surprising as it may be, Tunisia is the fourth largest producer in the world after Spain, Italy and Greece, and olive oil is Tunisia's foremost agricultural export. The average production is 120,000 tonnes per year of which 70,000 tonnes are exported. The olive oil industry in Tunisia also employs 20% of the population.

In Tunisia, they still harvest the olives by one of the most ancient methods. The picker covers every finger on the hand with a goat's horn, and using the hand like a rake, works down the branches of the trees. It is a method that has also given its name to a variety of olive, the Cornicabra.

About 800 BC, the Phoenicians voyaging to Spain set up permanent trading posts along the route. One of the most prosperous was Carthage and for the next three centuries they monopolised the sea routes, establishing the olive in what is now

Tunisia. When Carthage fell to the Romans in 201 BC, the cultivation of this valuable cash crop was extended further along the north coast into Algeria and Libya.

The olive is therefore well settled in this part of the world, and the Mediterranean climate ensures ideal growing conditions, but olive trees do not grow below 30° latitude in North Africa because of the Presaharan temperatures and almost non-existant rainfall. Above this latitude there is a wet season which lasts 4 or 5 months, November to the end of March and a dry season of 7 to 8 months, April to November.

The seasons and the extremes of temperature present the olive with particular difficulties in North Africa. Olive trees are especially temperature sensitive and there is a great danger in the autumn and winter of the unharvested fruit freezing; and in spring the flowers may be damaged by frosts. Moreover, there are often sudden falls in temperature in the winter which can destroy the whole crop as happened in Europe in the great freeze of 1956. The olive tree has a tendency to hibernate in prolonged cold and this dictates at what altitude the trees can be grown, but equally the plains can be susceptible to late frosts during the flowering season. The cold is, of course, not the only concern as high temperatures can cause damage at critical times — for example, a hot dry wind can burn the flowers off the trees in a matter of hours.

Hardy though the olive is, it needs to have some water and in North Africa, where the rain comes in abundance for 5 or 6 months, the trees can become swamped during the wet season. This has a similar effect to overwatering your indoor houseplants — the leaves yellow and die. For the rest of the year, the earth is baked by a relentless sun, causing a water deficiency. So careful attention has to be given to the rainfall levels and the soil. Heavy rain is not in itself harmful if the soil allows the rain to drain away, but if the soil is thin and the rain soaks away, then irrigation is needed and the development of this has been one great step forward in North African olive growing.

Incidentally, it is interesting to note when you visit any olive-growing region that the ground around the trees is well tilled and weeded. This is because any other plants compete with the tree for water.

Moroccan cuisine is a unique blend of many influences from over the centuries. The Phoenicians and Carthaginians travelled to Morocco and for a while it was part of the Roman Empire. When the Moors invaded Spain in the 9th century they found olive trees growing in Andalucia, and they brought back with them the Spanish habit of using olives and olive oil in their dishes. You will find olives used in the succulent Moroccan tagines — their famous, long slow simmered stews. Also in the delicious chicken with preserved lemons. But mostly in North Africa, because the olives are so tasty and varied, they are best appreciated as a snack in the cool shadows of a cafe, while you watch the hectic traffic of people, bicycles and animals throng the dusty streets.

CHICKEN WITH BROKEN OLIVES

 You can add preserved lemons to this dish if you have them. It's worth preparing some jars because they are used a great deal in Moroccan cooking and can also be sliced up and used in salads. They make colourful and unusual gifts as well.

To serve 4

1 chicken, approx 3lb	small bunch of parsley
1lb cracked green olives, stoned	pinch of powdered saffron
3tbs olive oil	$\frac{1}{2}$tsp cumin
$\frac{1}{2}$lb onions, sliced	$\frac{1}{2}$tsp mild paprika
$\frac{1}{2}$tsp ground ginger	salt and pepper, to taste
3 cloves of garlic, crushed	$2\frac{1}{2}$ cups water

Boil the olives in water for a few minutes and drain. Cut the chicken into serving pieces and place in a casserole with all the other ingredients except for the olives. Pour in the water. Cook, covered, over a low heat, turning the chicken from time to time, for about 45 minutes, adding more water if necessary. Then add the olives and cook for a further 15 minutes or until the chicken comes away easily from the bone. Remove the chicken from the pan and cook the sauce until it has thickened. Arrange the chicken pieces on a warm serving dish and pour the sauce over. If using preserved lemons, add the peel of one lemon at the same time as the olives.

PRESERVED LEMONS. Choose smooth, thin-skinned, unblemished lemons. Scrub them well. Make two vertical cuts in a cross to within about $\frac{1}{2}$ inch of their base, so that they still hold together. Put 1.25ml ($\frac{1}{4}$tsp) of salt into the centre of each lemon and press them closed. Pack tight in sterilized, glass jars. Sprinkle in 15ml (1tbs) of salt and the strained juice of a lemon. Top up the jar with boiling water and seal. Leave them for 3–4 weeks. To use them, rinse well under cold water and discard the flesh and pith, retaining peel only.

LAMB TAGINE WITH OLIVES

Tagines are the wonderful stews of Morocco and have the same name as their cooking pot. These earthenware dishes with conical lids come in every conceivable size from the tiny for one person to the vast for a banquet. The meal is cooked and served in its dish; as you lift the lid you are enveloped in the delicious aroma of lamb, chicken or fish combined with prunes, quince, coriander, cumin or ginger — the variations are endless.

To serve 4–6

3lb lamb, cut into cubes
2 onions, grated
2 cloves of garlic, chopped
handful of parsley, chopped
4tbs fresh coriander leaves,
    chopped

1tsp powdered ginger
1tsp ground cumin
$\frac{1}{3}$ cup olive oil
1 cup green olives
water
salt. to taste

Put all the ingredients except the olives into a bowl and let the lamb marinate overnight. Transfer the lamb and the marinade to a tagine or casserole. Add enough water to cover the meat and simmer over a low heat, covered for 1 hour or until the meat is tender. Put the olives into the casserole after about 45 minutes. To serve. arrange the meat on a warm serving dish and reduce the sauce until it is thick. Pour over the meat.

LAMB COUSCOUS

 Couscous is one of the great dishes of North Africa, cooked traditionally in a couscousier, which is a metal pan topped with a steamer and cover. The meat and vegetables cook in the bottom, while the couscous cooks in the top. You can improvise equally well with a sieve or colander on the top of a saucepan.

To serve 6

$2\frac{1}{2}$lb lamb	12oz turnips
2 large onions, sliced	8oz pumpkin
$\frac{1}{2}$tsp harissa	8oz courgettes
2tbs tomato puree	8oz chick peas, soaked
4tbs olive oil	salt and pepper, to taste
1lb couscous	water
1lb carrots	

Heat some olive oil in a pan and brown the onions. Add the meat, some salt and pepper, harissa and the tomato puree. Peel and wash the vegetables, cut them into pieces and add them all to the pan, except for the pumpkin and courgettes. Cover with cold water and bring to the boil. Put the coucous into a bowl and mix with 6 tbs of cold water and 2tbs of oil. Put this mixture into the top of the couscoussier and steam for 30 minutes. Remove the top half of the couscoussier, cover the lower half and simmer for at least 1 hour. Put the couscous into a bowl and break it up with the spoon, then run the grains through your hands to separate them. Sprinkle with a little cold water and fluff the grains again. Add the pumpkin and courgettes to the pan with the meat and vegetables, 30 minutes before serving. At the same time put the couscous back into the top of the pan and replace over the bottom half. Remove the couscous and mix in a bowl with butter and a little of the juices from the lower pan. Pile the couscous onto a serving dish, make a well in the centre and fill with the meat and vegetables. Serve the meat and vegetable juices separately.

HARISSA
(HOT CHILLI SAUCE)

This fiery sauce is a popular condiment in Tunisia, Morocco and Algeria, where it is used to accompany couscous, soups and stews. It will keep for months in a jar in the refrigerator if you cover the top of the sauce with a layer of olive oil.

4oz dried, red chilli peppers	$\frac{2}{3}$ cup olive oil
4 cloves of garlic	salt, to taste

Split the chillis and remove the stems and seeds. Soak the chillis in warm water for about an hour until they are soft. Put them in a mortar or blender, with the garlic and some salt. Pound to a paste, then add the olive oil gradually until you have a smooth sauce.

MOROCCAN ORANGE AND OLIVE SALAD

Oranges and lemons are used quite commonly in salads in Morocco, the lemon often being pickled first for a few weeks. Additions to this delicious and unusual salad can be finely sliced onion and fresh herbs like mint or marjoram. This dish is excellent served with the rich tagines found in Morocco or with roasted meat.

Serves 4

4 large oranges	2.5ml ($\frac{1}{2}$tsp) Dijon mustard
100g (4oz) black olives	Salt and freshly milled black
60ml (4tbs) olive oil	pepper
30ml (2tbs) Lemon Juice	

Peel the oranges and remove all the pith. Cut into thin slices and reserve any juice. Stone the olives and put the olives and oranges into a bowl. Put all the remaining ingredients including any orange juice into a screw-topped jar and shake until blended. Pour this mixture over the oranges and olives and toss well. Chill slightly before serving.

THE
AMERICAS

*T*he Carthaginians, Greeks and Romans introduced the olive into their 'New World', and in the same way when the Spanish missionaries ventured to Paraguay and Peru, in the 16th century, they brought the olive to South America, where it spread into Mexico and finally into California, which is now the main olive-growing area in the USA.

In world terms, olive oil produced in California is a drop in the ocean, somewhere between 0.4–0.5%! Moreover, the

California

development of the canning industry meant that olive growers in California decided long ago that it was more profitable to sell their olives for preserving, rather than go to the trouble of pressing them for oil. As a consequence, 95% of olives grown in California are canned.

But when the Americans apply themselves to age old crafts, you can be sure they will always come up with interesting new approaches. Californian wine-makers have, indeed, been showing all the European countries a thing or two in the last few years, and their real innovation has been to market their wines as varietals, which means calling the wine by the name of the grape.

This is exactly what Nick Sciabica of Modesto, in California's Central Valley, has introduced with his olive oils. You don't just buy a bottle of olive oil, which could be made up of a blend of two or three different olives, you buy a single variety olive oil. They grow the Mission variety, so-called because it was the variety introduced by the Spanish missionaries, the Manzanilla, and the Sevillano. All the cold pressed extra virgin oil they produce is sold under the name of the olive. They also market early harvest and late or fall harvest oils. This means going to the same trees twice, to pick at different stages of ripeness.

The result is olive oil of different flavours. Olives from the early harvest produce a fruity, dark green but slightly heavy oil. The later harvested olives yield a light, sweet, golden oil. The Mission olive produces a particularly delicious, fruity, sweet oil because the olives will continue to remain on the tree, sometimes into May. The Manzanilla and Sevillano on the other hand, have to be harvested before December or they will start to fall from the trees. Some Californian producers mix the early harvest oil and the late harvest oil for a finer balance.

Despite the enormous growth in olive oil consumption in the USA in the last few years, largely because of the health benefits, there are now only about six producers of olive oil in California, where once there were nearer seventy. Imports from Italy, France and Spain fill the demands of the consumers at prices that the domestic industry finds hard to match.

These olive oils from Spain, France and Italy are categorized according to acidity. In the USA they are divided into two

*Harvest time in
California*

categories, first pressed virgin or refined and blended (pure). This is a rather more sensible approach, because acidity can be reduced by chemical treatment. Therefore, if the only criteria for an extra virgin is its acidity, it is possible to treat it and market it as extra virgin providing its acidity is less than 1%. But if the label declares first pressed you know exactly what you are getting. American cooking is an accumulation and adaptation of every ethnic cuisine, going back as far as the plain English food of the Pilgrim Fathers. Because of this great variety of nationalities, American cooks have always been open to new influences and as such are some of the most innovative creators in the field of gastronomy, especially on the West coast, where a wealth of fresh produce is available. Traditional European and Eastern recipes form the basis for a range of specialities which can truly be termed American cuisine.

South American cuisine is a subject so vast and varied that to skate through it here will do it little justice. There is one definitive work on the subject, however, Elizabeth Lambert Ortiz's brilliant book, *Latin American Cooking*, and she has generously given me the benefit of her knowledge on the subject of the olive in this region of the world.

Introduced by the Spanish, olives have been absorbed into the staggering catalogue of ingredients used in all the South American countries. Corn and peppers feature regularly in many dishes, as does the abundant avocado — a fruit which we owe to the Mexicans, grown there as far back as 7000 BC. The Spanish brought the olive to Mexico and took back the tomato, which was grown by the Aztecs. The olive is not used much in the cooking of dishes, but it appears liberally as a garnish and is eaten much as they do in Greece as a snack.

I found it interesting to track the olive's journey to South America, because we think of it as the exclusive bounty of the Mediterranean. No so, olives grow with great success in Chile and Argentina, where there is a tree which is 400 years old, planted in the time of Charles III, and this well travelled fruit has been in South America just as long as its white settlers have.

GUACAMOLE
(AVOCADO DIP)

 This Mexican dish has become immensely popular, largely thanks to a plentiful supply of avocados all year round. There are a number of variations; you can add chilli, onion or chopped hard boiled egg. Serve it with crudities or tacos chips.

2 ripe avocados, peeled and stoned
1tbs lemon juice
2–4tbs olive oil
1 clove of garlic, crushed

1tsp fresh coriander leaves, chopped
1 large tomato, peeled, seeded and chopped
salt and pepper, to taste

Mash together or blend the avocados and lemon juice. Then mix in the garlic, coriander, olive oil and tomato. Season to taste.

PICADILLO
(MINCED BEEF WITH OLIVES AND RAISINS)

 This is a traditional Mexican dish which can be served with rice as a supper dish or it can be used to fill tortillas and empanadas.

To serve 4–6

2lb minced beef
3tbs olive oil
1 large onion, chopped
1 clove of garlic, chopped
14oz canned, peeled tomatoes
2tbs tomato puree
2 green chillis, chopped

½ cup raisins
10 stuffed olives, sliced
½tsp ground cinnamon
salt and pepper, to taste
⅔ cup blanched almonds, toasted

Heat the oil in a large pan. Add the onion and garlic and cook until they are soft. Stir in the meat and cook until it is browned. Stir in all the remaining ingredients except the almonds, bring to the boil and then lower heat and simmer for about 40 minutes. Before serving scatter over the almonds.

SEVICHE
(MARINATED RAW FISH)

 This South American dish has now become very popular as the fashion for raw fish has spread. You can treat almost any fish in this way but the best to use are plaice, sole, and salmon. The fish must, however, be as fresh as possible.

To serve 4

1lb of fish or mixed fish
lemon juice or lime juice
1 onion, chopped

1 clove of garlic
1 dried hot red chilli, crumbled
6tbs olive oil

Cut the fish into strips or thin slices and cover completely with the lemon or lime juice. Refrigerate for at least 3 hours. Drain off the juice and use some of it to make a dressing with the rest of the ingredients. Pour the dressing over the fish, refrigerate again for a couple of hours and serve at room temperature.

*Provincial home,
South America*

SAUTEED MONKFISH WITH RED PEPPER MAYONNAISE

The Americans have taken up the new, lighter style of cooking and a good number of their recipes make original and imaginative use of olive oil. This recipe uses both pure and extra virgin oil, the pure for its mild flavour in the cooking and the stronger, extra virgin for fruitiness in the sauce.

To serve 4

1lb monkfish
½ cup olive oil, pure
1 red pepper, deseeded and
   chopped
1 egg yolk

1 clove of garlic
⅔ cup olive oil, extra virgin
salt and pepper, to taste
lemon wedges
parsley, chopped for garnish

Remove any membrane from the fish and slice into neat medallions. Season with salt and pepper. Heat the pure olive oil in a pan, add the fish and brown on all sides. Cook until tender.

Puree the pepper in a blender until completely smooth. Remove and squeeze out any excess water in doubled kitchen towel. Put the garlic and egg yolk in a blender and process, gradually add the olive oil. Add enough red pepper puree to the blender to colour the mixture and according to your taste. Serve the fish with the mayonnaise and garnish with lemon wedges and a sprinkling of parsley.

OLIVE OIL HERB DRESSING

The Americans probably have more salad dressings than any other nation! This tangy dressing can be served in the summer as soon as fresh herbs are available, with any vegetable or green salads as well as with seafood.

large bunch of parsley
handful of chives, chopped
1 clove of garlic
2tbs Dijon mustard

scant 1 cup olive oil
$\frac{1}{4}$ cup red wine vinegar
3tbs lemon juice
salt and pepper, to taste

Place all the ingredients in a blender and process until smooth. Season to taste.

ORANGE ALMOND FIG CAKE

This recipe from the United States is an unusual and delicious dessert with a definite flavour of the Mediterranean and shows how well olive oil can be used in cakes.

10 dried figs, finely chopped
2tbs flour
2 eggs
$\frac{2}{3}$ cup olive oil
scant 1 cup granulated sugar
4 cups flour
$\frac{1}{2}$tsp cinnamon

$1\frac{1}{2}$tsp baking powder
$\frac{3}{4}$ cup ground almonds
$\frac{1}{4}$tsp salt
$\frac{2}{3}$ cup fresh orange juice
zest of 1 orange, finely minced
$\frac{1}{3}$ cup sliced almonds

Preheat the oven to 180°C (350°F), Gas Mark 4. Toss the chopped figs in the 30ml (2tbs) of flour. Beat the eggs, olive oil and sugar until you have a thick, creamy mixture. Mix the flour with the cinnamon, baking powder, ground almonds and salt. Add the flour mixture alternatively with the orange juice to the egg mixture, stirring until blended. Stir in the orange zest and chopped figs. Grease an 8″ ring mould. Pour the batter into the mould and sprinkle with the sliced almonds. Bake for 35 minutes or until a cocktail stick inserted, comes out dry.

THE REST OF THE WORLD

*T*urkey, Portugal, Israel, Iraq, Iran, Albania, Yugoslavia, Australia, South Africa, Jordan and Syria all grow olives. To lump them all together and not mention them individually, in detail is not to diminish their significance or to suggest that the olive industries in these countries are not sometimes as highly developed as that of the Mediterranean. We must remember that amongst these countries, Syria is the one which history indicates, first grew the olive and exported its oil to the rest of the known world. Also that Turkey ranks in the top five of the world's producers.

It is merely that the oil from these places does not find its way onto the shelves of our stores. This is usually because the total production is consumed domestically and also because in some cases the growers are small, peasant farmers who are not able to market their oil abroad.

In Portugal for example, olives are grown in the Alentejo region, an expanse of arid, sun-baked earth in the South and the port producing areas of Tras-os-Montes and the Alto Douro. It is amazing that anything grows in these last two areas. The sheer mountains are solid slate and granite and in the summer the temperatures soar. The vines, cork trees and olive trees here are planted on terraces carved and in some cases blasted out of the mountain sides. Obviously in this terrain mechanization of any kind is impossible, and even transportation, once the olives are picked, is a problem.

Many of the port producers grow olives, but they have always been regarded as a secondary crop. As the demand for extra virgin oils has begun to increase, they are now beginning to turn their attention to the possible sales overseas. The port shippers are in an ideal position to market their own olive oils because they already have the channels of distribution for their wines. I predict that we will be seeing more Portuguese oils appearing in the shops before too long.

At the moment, there is only one Portuguese olive oil I know of which is marketed internationally. This is Villaflor. It is a pale golden oil, with a fruity flavour and delicate aroma, made from Cordovil, Verdeal and Madural olives. Robert Kruger, the power behind the marketing of this brand, believes that the olive oil industry is in a similar situation to the wine industry 20 years ago, with plenty of people selling the product but no one marketing it. I agree with him that when the consumer is more' educated' and experimental, the demand will grow.

The burgeoning curiosity about the olive and its history has been met in Israel by the recent founding of a magnificent oil industry museum at Haifa. The exhibits cover the ancient methods of production right up to the present day. There is a restored lever and screw press from the Byzantine period, in the museum's courtyard and during the olive harvest, visitors can produce oil by operating these reconstructed presses. A garden of all sorts of oil-giving plants includes various types of olive trees. Inside the museum there are fascinating displays of everything to do with olive oil — coins and artefacts, ointments and soaps as well as photographs and plans of ancient sites which have been excavated in the country. At one site, Tel Miqne, which was the biblical city of Ekron, 100 olive press complexes have been uncovered. It has been calculated that this town in about the 9th century BC was producing 500,000 litres of olive oil per year!

As more archaeological research, of the sort being undertaken in Israel, progresses, we shall perhaps uncover some of the mysteries which still remain about the origins of the olive but then all good mysteries have some questions that always remain unanswered. That is part of their eternal fascination.

AVOCADO AND GRAPEFRUIT SALAD

I often serve this unusual combination which comes from the Middle East, as a light starter. The oiliness of the avocados contrasts well with the acidity of the fruit.

2 large ripe avocados
2 grapefruit
juice of 1 lemon

$\frac{1}{4}$ cup olive oil
salt and pepper, to taste

Prepare the dressing with some lemon juice, olive oil, salt and pepper. Peel and slice the avocados and drop immediately into the dressing. Peel the grapefruit and remove all the pith. Divide into segments and cut each segment in half, add to the avocado and toss well. Chill and serve.

IMAM BAYALDI
(STUFFED AUBERGINES)

This is one of the classic dishes of Turkey. The name actually means 'The Iman fainted', supposedly at the amount of olive oil used!

To serve 4 as a main dish, 8 as a starter

4 medium-sized aubergines
$\frac{2}{3}$ cup olive oil
2 large onions, sliced
3 cloves of garlic, chopped

4 large tomatoes, peeled
handful of parsley, chopped
salt and pepper, to taste
nutmeg, to taste

Cut the aubergines in half lengthways, scoop out a little of the flesh to make room for the filling, sprinkle the insides and the reserved flesh with salt, set aside for about 15 minutes. Meanwhile heat 5tbs of olive oil in a pan, add the onions and garlic, and saute until soft and golden. Stir in the tomatoes, parsley and seasoning and cook for a further 5 minutes. Heat the rest of the olive oil in a pan and fry the aubergine flesh for a few minutes and add to the tomato mixture. Fry the aubergine halves in the same pan, until the flesh softens, adding more oil if necessary. Arrange the aubergines in a baking dish and spoon on the stuffing. Pour $2\frac{1}{2}$ cups of boiling water into the dish, cover and simmer on a low heat until the aubergines are cooked, about 1 hour. They can be served hot or cold.

FISH KEBABS

Turkey is famed for its kebabs, both fish and meat, which are usually marinated before cooking in a mixture of olive oil and lemon juice with the addition of various aromatics. This tenderizes and flavours. Swordfish is one of the best fish for this type of treatment because the flesh is firm and in Turkey it is traditionally served with Tarator sauce.

To serve 4

2lb swordfish
1 onion, grated
⅔ cup olive oil
juice of 1 lemon

bay leaves
salt and pepper, to taste
wedges of lemon

Cut the fish into 1" cubes. Put the onion, lemon juice, olive oil, salt and pepper into a large bowl, add the fish and stir well to coat with the marinade. Leave for at least an hour. Remove the fish from the marinade and thread onto skewers, alternating a bay leaf between each cube of fish. Cook the kebabs over a charcoal fire for about 10 minutes, brushing them from time to time with the marinade. Serve with wedges of lemon and Tarator (Walnut) sauce.

Turkish fishermen

TARATOR SAUCE

1 cup walnuts
2 cloves of garlic
1 slice of white bread, crusts
    removed and soaked in water

juice of 1 lemon
⅔ cup olive oil
salt, to taste

Grind the walnuts, garlic and salt in a blender or mortar. Then add the bread, squeezed dry. Add half the lemon juice and slowly add the olive oil until you have a thick, smooth sauce. Add more lemon juice according to taste.

CALDO VERDE
(CABBAGE SOUP)

Like many of the soups of Italy, this one is served at the table with a jug of olive oil. In Portugal, caldo verde is made with a large cabbage known as *couve* but it can be made with green cabbage. The cabbage must be sliced very finely because it is barely cooked.

To serve 6

1lb potatoes
1lb green cabbage, finely sliced
water

2tbs olive oil
salt, to taste

Peel and cook the potatoes in just enough salted water to cover them. Blend the potatoes with their cooking water. Thin with more water if necessary, you should have a medium consistency. Add the cabbage and the olive oil. Cook uncovered for 5 minutes, until the cabbage is lightly cooked, it should be a little crisp. Serve with a jug of olive oil.

CAMAROES GRELHADO
(GRILLED PRAWNS)

With its lengthy coastline, fish and shellfish are in abundant supply in Portugal and mostly the seafood is cooked very simply, on a grill over charcoal. The flavour of fish, fresh from the day's catch and grilled over an open fire is something to be savoured.

To serve 4

1lb fresh prawns
3 cloves of garlic, crushed
½inch fresh ginger

juice of ½ lemon
4tbs olive oil
1 fresh green chilli

Blend together all the ingredients except the prawns. Marinate them in the mixture for at least two hours. Drain the prawns, reserving the marinade, and grill for about 10–15 minutes, basting the whole time with the marinade. Serve with wedges of lemon and bread to mop up the juices.

BACALAU A GOMES DE SA

(SALT COD WITH POTATOES, ONIONS AND OLIVES)

Salt cod is cooked all along the Mediterranean. Some people say that there is a recipe for salt cod for each day of the year! I had it a number of years ago in Portugal as a cold starter and was immediately hooked. It is a bit time consuming to prepare and needs plenty of soaking but is well worth the effort.

To serve 4

1½lb salt cod
2lb potatoes
1¼ cups olive oil
2 large onions

1 clove of garlic, chopped
20 black olives, stoned
4 hard boiled eggs, sliced
parsley, chopped for garnish

Start preparation the day before you want to eat the dish. Cover the salt cod with water and soak overnight, changing the water three or four times.

Preheat the oven to 200°C (400°F), Gas Mark 6. Drain the cod and rinse in cold water, place in a pan with sufficient water to cover. Bring to the boil and then simmer just under boiling point for 20 minutes or until the fish flakes easily. Drain the fish and remove any bones and skin, then flake the flesh. Peel the potatoes and cook in boiling, salted water until just tender. Drain and slice. Heat a good measure of olive oil in a pan and cook the garlic and onion until soft but not brown. Grease a baking dish with olive oil. Spread a layer of half the potatoes over the bottom of the dish, cover them with half the cod and then half the onions. Repeat the layers with the rest of the potatoes, cod and onions. Pour the remaining olive oil over the top and bake for about 20 minutes. Garnish with the sliced hard boiled eggs, olives and parsley.

Salt cod in Portugal

FRANGO PIRI-PIRI
(CHICKEN PIRI-PIRI)

When I first went to Portugal a few years ago I knew nothing of the food and rather expected it to be similar to Spanish cuisine. I was on the south coast well away from the tourist haunts and sampled different local specialities, every day. The cooking was a great revelation, I had some wonderful meals and needless to say the seafood was splendid. In one lovely old Roman town, there was a little family run restaurant, where they served the best chicken I have ever tasted. It was cooked over a charcoal fire but I was fascinated by the olive oil mixture it was basted with. The owner rushed into the kitchen and came back with a jar of olive oil packed with dried red chilli peppers. He explained that this concoction was Piri-Piri. You can quite easily make this yourself and use it when barbequeing or roasting chicken.

To make Piri-Piri

Take a sealable, glass jar and fill a third of the jar with dried red chilli peppers. Pour in sufficient olive oil to fill the jar. Seal and leave for a few weeks.

To serve 4

1 chicken	juice of $\frac{1}{2}$ lemon
salt, to taste	Piri-Piri

Rub the outside of the chicken with salt and sprinkle over some lemon juice and leave it to stand for about 30 minutes. Preheat the oven to 180°C (350°F), Gas Mark 4. Brush the chicken with Piri-Piri and cook for about 1 hour or until the chicken is done. Baste it occasionally with more piri-piri, while it is cooking.

OLIVE OIL IN THE SHOPS

During the research and writing of this book, I have sampled nearly 50 extra virgin oils, ranging in price from under £2.00 a bottle to over £12.00. I discovered that generally you get what you pay for — the more expensive the oil, the better the quality. Sadly out of all the oils tasted, I found a great number of very bland or bad tasting oils. Listed below are some of my personal favourites.

SUPERMARKET BRANDS

Many people starting to use olive oil will probably pick up their first bottle in their local supermarket. There is no question that the extra virgins they sell are exceptionally cheap but I have found most of them to be disappointing, with flavours untypical of good olive oil. Many sell olive oil in plastic bottles, and in some cases I could detect a chemical backtaste which may or may not be from the bottle.

The one supermarket brand I really liked, interestingly comes in a glass bottle and is from Waitrose. This is a green gold extra virgin from Italy, with a very pleasant green leaf aroma and almond flavour, at an amazing price.

NATIONAL BRANDS

These are the olive oils produced by large companies and the ones you most commonly find on the shelves. Of the Italian brands, I think that Sasso extra virgin is the tastiest, it has a fresh olive smell with a green leaf taste. It is also exceedingly good value for money.

One of my most favourite olive oils and one I use a lot is Carbonell extra virgin from Spain. It is a richly fruity oil and is delicious for cooking and salads.

SINGLE ESTATE OLIVE OILS

These are the oils at the top end of the market in both quality and price. They are the 'premier crus' and if you really want to discover what a fine olive oil should taste like you should treat yourself to a bottle of any of the following.

ITALY

Without question one of the best extra virgins from Italy is Fattoria Dell'Ugo, a light emerald green oil from Tuscany, with a lovely aroma of apples and a light peppery taste.

Equally I enjoy Olio Extra Vergine Di Oliva Della Riviera Ligure from Leonardo Raineri, a golden oil from Liguria with a light olive aroma and fruity, grassy flavour. Raineri also produce a Olio Extra Vergine Di Oliva, which is a pale gold with a light fresh taste and one which I think would be excellent for making mayonnaise, because it does not have an over-powering flavour.

From the Abruzzo region of Italy, an olive oil produced by Santagata is well balanced and fruity, golden in colour.

Some other exceedingly fine Italian extra virgins to look out for are Badia a Coltibuono, Tenuto Carpazo, from Montalcino, Castello di Almonte from Umbria, and Colonna from the Molise region of central Italy.

FRANCE

Most of the French oils I tasted did not impress me, but it is only fair to say that there are few available in the shops and the best French oils are not available outside France. However Henri Bellon, who incidentally is the mayor of Fontvieille, produces a pale green, sweet fruity olive oil.

SPAIN

I personally like the style of Spanish olive oils very much. They are fruity and fragrant, without the peppery taste you get in some of the Italian oils. Two which are excellent are Lerida and Sierra de Segura from the Cooperativa Santa Ana.

GREECE

Some of the Greek style olive oils are wonderfully strong and fruity. My favourite is Sparta, made with organically grown olives.

WORLD PRODUCTION (1980/81)

COUNTRY	NO OF OLIVE TREES (MILLIONS)	OIL (1000 TONS) PROD	EXPORT	IMPORT	TABLE OLIVES (1000 TONS) PROD	EXPORT	IMPORT
Spain	193	416	92	–	151	78	–
Italy	183	407	17	95	74	2	22
Greece	113	211	20	–	63	40	–
Turkey	80	108	15	–	125	3	–
Tunisia	56	116	64	–	7	0.6	–
Portugal	50	42	2	2	2	20	–
Morocco	27	28	10	–	45	31	–
Syrian A.R.	20.4	47	–	–	32.6	–	–
Algeria	20	11.6	–	–	6.8	2.5	–
Argentina	5	30	4.8	60	64	20	–
France	4	1.7	6	26	2.4	2.5	27
USA	2.2	0.6	–	25	62	2	39.5

OIL AND FAT COMPOSITIONS

FOOD	% SATURATED	% MONO-SATURATED	% POLY-UNSATURATED
Coconut oil	92	6	2
Olive oil	12	80	8
Corn oil	16	27	57
Sunflower oil	10	18	72
Safflower oil	12	10	78
Butter	58	39	3
Margarine	64	30	6

INDEX
Recipes

Varieties of Olive

GENERAL INDEX

*Numbers in italic refer to
illustrations*

The list below gives some American equivalents or substitutes for terms and ingredients used in this book:

British	American
frying pan	skillet
greaseproof paper	wax paper
grill	broil
grill (noun)	broiler
piping bag	pastry bag
stoned	pitted
hard-boiled eggs	hard-cooked eggs
black olives	ripe olives
prawns, peeled	shrimp, shelled
tomato purée	tomato paste
cornflour	cornstarch
courgettes	zucchini
aubergines	eggplants
fresh yeast	compressed yeast
dried yeast	active dry yeast
spring onions	scallions
short crust pastry	basic pie dough
fresh coriander	cilantro
topside of beef	top round of beef
minced beef	ground beef
monkfish	angler fish

France

Liguria

Provence

Lerida

Corsica

Portugal

Spain

Italy

Umb

Sardinia

Andalucia

Sici

Tunisia

Morocco

Algeria